HIGH-FLAVOR, LOW-FAT DESSERTS

Steven Raichlen's

HIGH-FLAVOR, LOW-FAT DESSERTS

Photography by Greg Schneider

VIKING

VIKING
Published by the Penguin Group
Penguin Books USA Inc., 375 Hudson Street,
New York, New York 10014, U.S.A.
Penguin Books Ltd, 27 Wrights Lane,
London W8 5TZ, England
Penguin Books Australia Ltd, Ringwood,
Victoria, Australia
Penguin Books Canada Ltd, 10 Alcorn Avenue,
Toronto, Ontario, Canada M4V 3B2
Penguin Books (N.Z.) Ltd, 182–190 Wairau Road,
Auckland 10, New Zealand

Penguin Books Ltd, Registered Offices:
Harmondsworth, Middlesex, England

First published in 1997 by Viking Penguin,
a division of Penguin Books USA Inc.

1 3 5 7 9 10 8 6 4 2

Copyright © Steven Raichlen, 1997
Photographs copyright © Greg Schneider, 1997
All rights reserved

LIBRARY OF CONGRESS CATALOGING-IN-PUBLICATION DATA
Raichlen, Steven.
[High-flavor, low-fat desserts]
Steven Raichlen's high-flavor, low-fat desserts.
p.   cm.
Includes index.
ISBN 0-670-87136-2
1. Desserts.   2. Low-fat diet—Recipes.   I. Title.
TX773.R197   1997
641.8′6—dc20   96-22120

This book is printed on acid-free paper.

Printed in the United States of America
Set in Goudy
Designed by Katy Riegel

*This book is dedicated with love
to the sweetest person on earth,
my Grammie Ethel!*

ACKNOWLEDGMENTS

This may be a little book, but it took a lot of work on the part of many people.

First, I want to thank my recipe testers: Elida Proenza, Cathy Peplowski, Kevin Pierce, and Magda Queimado. We all mourn Magda's tragic death and will miss her. Her spirit lives on in her lovely daughter, Mariana.

Once again, Greg Schneider has brought my recipes to life with his stunning photographs and irrepressible spirit. He was assisted by the ever-cheerful Michael Donnelly. Debbie Cheleotis provided logistical support in the office. Karen Brasel did the nutritional analyses. A big thanks to Scotty's Grocery.

Dawn Drzal at Viking Penguin graced the manuscript with her expert editing. I'd like to thank all my friends at Viking for their enthusiasm and support, including Barbara Grossman, Cathy Hemming, Norm Sheinman, Paul Slovak, Patti Kelly, and Elizabeth Riley.

Above all, I want to thank my family, especially the kids—Jake, Betsy, and Mark—who showed remarkable forbearance when it came to not eating the food destined for photography. And, of course, my wife, Barbara, who survived yet another photo shoot (and yet another promise that it would be the last) and whose love and support made this—and all my endeavors—possible.

PHOTO CREDITS

My heartfelt thanks to the following for providing props and accessories:

Delores "DJ" Sticht and Dusty Weiss, of Burdines.

Yvette Kalinowsky, of Iberia Tiles.

Stephanie Aronson, potter.

Manuel Ruvuelta, artist.

CONTENTS

INTRODUCTION

Is there any sweeter word in the English language than "dessert"? Unfortunately, the last course of a meal is fraught with nutritional peril. Even the most health-conscious among us feel our resolve waver before a table heaped with fattening desserts. While there's nothing intrinsically evil about eggs, cream, or butter when consumed in moderation, moderation can be hard to manage when it comes time for dessert.

But what if you could prepare your favorite desserts using only a fraction of the fat found in traditional recipes?

That's exactly what I've tried to do in this, the sixth book of the High-Flavor, Low-Fat cookbook series: create a wide range of desserts that aren't just good for you but are great-looking and great-tasting, too.

Writing this book has taken me for a stroll down memory lane. The year was 1976; the place, the Ecole de Cuisine La Varenne in Paris. It was at the legendary French cooking school that I learned the art of baking and dessert making. Back then, chefs used butter, cream, and eggs with abandon. No one worried much about cholesterol and counting fat grams.

For more than a decade, I prepared the dessert recipes I learned to make in Paris. But as North Americans became more health-conscious, and as my own cholesterol level rose, I gradually abandoned the preparations I once considered crucial to a basic culinary education. As a matter of fact, I greatly curtailed my dessert consumption. And when I did indulge, I came to prefer simple fruit desserts.

The writing of this book has brought me back to my French culinary roots. For if the ingredients have changed, the basic techniques remain the same: the proper way to cook crepes, make meringues, roll out pastry dough. It's the soundness of these basic techniques that has enabled me to discover the substitutions that make High-Flavor, Low-Fat desserts possible.

High-Flavor, Low-Fat dessert making requires a new approach to ingredients. Eggs are among the worst of the offenders. Fortunately, there are two sides to an egg: the yolk and the white. The yolks give custards their golden glow and firm consistency, but the whites have the same ability to set custards and other creamy desserts without the fat.

Besides, consumed in moderation, eggs provide useful nutrients. Egg whites are almost pure protein. So are egg substitutes, of which egg whites are the main ingredient. When you use only whites, however, you lose some of the richness imparted by whole eggs or egg yolks. By enhancing the whites with spices and other seasonings, you can create a different sort of richness: the fragrance of fresh vanilla and lemon zest; the tongue-tingling tang of candied ginger, cardamom, and freshly grated nutmeg. My basic strategy is to retain one or two whole eggs or egg yolks for richness and substitute fat-free whites for the remainder. In many recipes I offer a range of eggs. In others, I make them optional: use them or not, depending on what your fat budget allows.

Another set of culprits are the baking fats: butter, oil, and solid vegetable shortening. Some years ago, health-minded bakers discovered that you could replace part of, or even all, the oil or butter in baked goods with puréed fruit, such as applesauce and prune purée. Fruit purées give pastries the same moist mouth feel as butter or shortening but without the noisome fat. Applesauce works well in light-colored baked goods like oatmeal cookies and fruit breads, while prune purée and apple butter do a fine job in brownies, chocolate cakes, and other chocolate desserts.

That's not to say I've completely eliminated oil and butter. You can't make crisp pastries or pie crusts without a little baking fat, and without these ingredients cakes and tea breads would be rubbery or leaden. I've tried to give a range of fat: if your fat budget allows, use the upper end; if you're on a strict low-fat diet, use the minimum.

Please note that when I do use butter—in filo-dough pastries, for example—I try to pair it with a more nutritionally beneficial fat, such as olive or canola oil. Often I'll lightly brush the outside of a pastry with melted butter and use oil inside. This tricks the palate: if the first thing you taste is butter, your taste buds may perceive butter throughout.

This brings us to one of America's favorite dessert ingredients: chocolate. Chocoholics will be relieved to know that they needn't eliminate the object of their passion entirely. The bulk of chocolate's flavor resides not in the fat-laden cocoa butter but in the cocoa powder. (This is why white chocolate, which consists largely of cocoa butter, has so little chocolate flavor.) Thus, cocoa powder makes an ideal flavoring for health-conscious chocoholics. To round out the flavor of cocoa, I often use vanilla and complementary spices such as cinnamon and cloves.

Even dairy products aren't as forbidden as they once were—not with the advent of nonfat yogurt and low- and no-fat sour cream and cottage cheese. Nonfat yogurt can be drained to make a tangy, fat-free cheese that's ideal for fillings. Nonfat sour cream can be boiled without curdling and is perfect for making icings and ice creams. Low- and no-fat cottage cheese can be puréed and used as a base for cheesecake.

One of the best ways to avoid fat is to base desserts on fruit. In the past decade, the growing availability of tropical and other exotic fruits has revolutionized the dessert maker's art. When I started out in this business, you were lucky to be able to find Comice pears or fresh raspberries. Today, most supermarkets carry pineapples, papayas, and mangoes, while gourmet shops routinely carry such exotic fruits as cherimoya and star fruit.

This book contains forty of my favorite High-Flavor, Low-Fat dessert recipes—cookies and cakes, pastries and soufflés, airy meringues and dark, rich chocolate confections. It's certainly a long way from the butter-and-egg days of Paris.

Who said you can't have your cake and eat it, too?

ABOUT INGREDIENTS

It's a well-known truth that a cook is only as good as his ingredients. One of the keys to successful High-Flavor, Low-Fat dessert making is to use the right raw materials.

EGGS AND EGG WHITES: When eggs or egg whites are called for in this book, they are always large ones. One large egg white is about 1 fluid ounce, so 1 large egg white equals about 2 tablespoons, and there are 8 large egg whites to 1 cup. Armed with this knowledge, you can adapt any size egg to these recipes.

HOW TO SEPARATE EGGS: When you separate eggs for beating, it's important that the whites be entirely free of yolk, since even a trace of fat will prevent the whites from whipping properly. I recommend separating the eggs one by one into two small bowls, one for the white and one for the yolk, then adding each successfully separated white to the mixing bowl. That way, you'll never have to throw away more than one white. (There's nothing worse than having 11 clean whites for an angel food cake and then ruining the whole batch with yolk from the twelfth. If you do get a bit of yolk in the whites, scoop it out with the edge of a broken shell. The shell contains an enzyme that cuts through the whites.) For the best results, have the whites at room temperature and be sure the bowl and beaters are completely dry and free of grease.

HOW TO BEAT EGG WHITES WITH AN ELECTRIC MIXER: Start beating the whites at low speed to break them up. Add cream of tartar or another acid, such as vinegar or lemon juice (½ teaspoon for 4 whites), and increase the speed to medium. Gradually increase the speed and beat the whites until they form soft peaks. If the recipe calls for sugar, add it now, and continue beating until the whites are firm and glossy but not dry, 6 to 8 minutes in all. Do not overbeat egg whites, or they will lose their resiliency and leavening power.

EGG SUBSTITUTES: This brings us to the subject of egg substitutes. This book and *High-Flavor, Low-Fat Appetizers* are the first of my books in which these products make an appearance. The purist in me still hesitates to use them, and they are given as an alternative to fresh. But the fact is that the main ingredient in egg substitutes is egg white, and they do a fine job of setting custards and pie fillings with no appreciable sacrifice in taste. On the downside, egg substitutes do contain preservatives and other additives and sodium.

WHAT TO DO WITH ALL THE LEFTOVER EGG YOLKS: High-Flavor, Low-Fat dessert making is bound to leave you with lots of egg yolks. Here are some ideas for what to do with them.

1. Feed them to a pet. (To be on the safe side, you may wish to cook them first to kill any salmonella.) According to veterinarians, the high lecithin content of egg yolk gives man's best friend a lustrous, shiny coat.

2. Add them to shampoo. The lecithin in egg yolk is said to give your hair strength and sheen.

3. Prepare a batch of paint. Tempera (an egg yolk–based paint) was the primary paint medium in late-medieval Europe. More recently, Andrew Wyeth used tempera to achieve the incredible detail in his work. Tempera is made by mixing one part egg yolk with two parts water and dry pigment. For complete instructions, consult *The Materials and Techniques of Medieval Painting*, by Daniel V. Thompson (Dover Books).

BREAD AND COOKIE CRUMBS: Bread crumbs, cookie crumbs, and graham-cracker crumbs are a valuable ally in the fight against fat. I like to sprinkle bread crumbs between sheets of filo dough to create crisp crusts with reduced fat. Cookie and graham-cracker crumbs can be used to make pie crusts with considerably less fat than a traditional pastry shell.

For the best results, use lightly toasted homemade bread crumbs. To make them, grind dry stale bread (store it in the freezer until you have enough to make a batch) in a food processor. Spread the crumbs in a thin layer on a baking sheet and toast in a 400-degree oven until golden brown.

To make cookie or graham-cracker crumbs, coarsely crumble them into the bowl of a food processor and grind to a powder. I particularly like crumbs made with cinnamon graham crackers.

FLOUR: Two types of flour are used in this book: unbleached all-purpose white flour and cake flour. Cake flour is milled from softer wheat than all-purpose flour and contains less gluten. It produces an exceptionally delicate consistency in cakes, roulades, and pastries. Do not use self-rising cake flour, which contains added baking powder.

FILO DOUGH: Popular in Greece and throughout the Middle East, filo consists of paper-thin sheets of flour-and-water dough. Once stretched out by hand, it is now made by machine. Filo dough is generally sold frozen in long, slender 1-pound boxes and is available in most supermarkets and gourmet shops; good brands include Krinos and Apollo. If you live in an area with a large Greek or Middle Eastern community, you may be able to find fresh filo dough. A 1-pound box contains 20 to 25 sheets. The most common size, and the one called for in this book, is 14 × 18 inches.

Filo dough is easy to work with, but there are a few things to watch for. Be sure to thaw frozen filo dough slowly in the refrigerator overnight, as rapid thawing will cause the sheets to stick together. Remove the dough from the package and count out the number of sheets you need, plus a few extra to allow for breakage.

Place the filo sheets on a work surface covered with plastic wrap. Place a piece of plastic wrap on top of the filo and cover it with a damp dishcloth. (Wrap any unused dough in foil with the ends tightly sealed and refrigerate.) Keep the sheets of filo covered until the last possible moment to keep them from drying out.

WONTON AND EGGROLL WRAPPERS: Wonton and eggroll wrappers are made with flour, water, and shortening or oil. Eggroll wrappers are larger —6- to 8-inch squares. Wonton wrappers are small squares, 3 to 4 inches on a side. Look for them in the produce section of your supermarket or in Asian markets. (They are also sold frozen in Asian markets.) Their use is perhaps the most revolutionary technique I've discovered for High-Flavor, Low-Fat baking. Chinese wonton and eggroll wrappers can be used to make pies and tartlets and even cannoli.

The wrappers are pressed into lightly oiled molds, lightly brushed with butter or sprayed with oil, and baked. This produces a hard, crisp crust with very little fat.

BUTTER: Butter is called for occasionally in this book, but I use it more as a flavoring than as a baking fat. When I make filo pastries, for example, I brush the dough with equal parts melted butter and olive oil. Another trick is to brush the outside of a pie crust or cannoli shells with melted butter: the first thing you taste will be butter, and as we said above, it will leave you with the overall impression of a richer dish. If possible, use unsalted butter.

OIL: All oils contain fat, but some oils are higher in monounsaturated fats, which promote "good" cholesterol, and lower in harmful saturated fats. The best oils from this perspective are canola and olive oil. You'll want to use an olive oil marked "light" or simply "olive oil," as an extra-virgin would have too strong a flavor for desserts.

SPRAY OIL: When I think of all the hours I spent laboriously brushing tart pans and baking sheets with melted butter, it's a wonder I didn't discover the eminently convenient and easy-to-use spray oils earlier. These are revolutionary products, enabling you to oil molds and even pastries using much less fat than before.

SOUR CREAM: Nonfat sour cream has virtually the same flavor and texture as regular sour cream. I use it or low-fat sour cream almost exclusively.

COTTAGE CHEESE: While fat-free cottage cheese is available, you'll get better results in your cooking if you use 1- or 2-percent cottage cheese. For firmer fillings and cheesecakes, drain cottage cheese overnight in the refrigerator using a yogurt strainer or a sieve lined with several layers of cheesecloth or paper towels and set over a bowl.

YOGURT CHEESE: Deliciously tart and creamy, yogurt cheese has become a mainstay of my High-Flavor, Low-Fat dessert making. It's easy to make, but you need to remember to put it in the refrigerator to drain ahead of time—ideally the night before. Drain the yogurt using a yogurt strainer or a sieve lined with several layers of cheesecloth or paper towels in the refrigerator set over a bowl to collect the whey, which you can drink. (Afghans mix it with soda water, dried mint, and salt or sugar to make a refreshing drink called *dooh*.)

CHOCOLATE: As little as an ounce of unsweetened chocolate will add a wonderful flavor to puddings and icings. Baker's brand chocolate works fine for everyday dessert making, but if you want really extraordinary results, use Valrhona or Callebaut. My favorite cocoa powder is Droste, from Holland.

The expression "Dutch-processed" refers to a cocoa that has been alkalized. It is less acidic and more flavorful than "natural" or "nonalkalized" cocoa. Droste and Lindt are the two most widely available brands of "Dutched" cocoa.

NUTS: Nuts are of limited use in High-Flavor, Low-Fat dessert making because they're loaded with fat. I use nuts sparingly, as a flavoring, and I always toast them in the oven to intensify their flavor. When you grind nuts in a food processor, run the machine in short bursts, as overgrinding will reduce nuts to an oily paste.

SPICES: Spices are essential to High-Flavor, Low-Fat dessert making. Whenever possible, I try to use whole spices, since once spices are ground they lose flavor rapidly. For example, I use cinnamon sticks and whole cloves to flavor syrups and pastry creams. Commercially ground spices are fine for cake batters and pastries, though you should try to grate nutmeg yourself.

LEMON AND ORANGE ZEST: The zest is the oil-rich outer skin of a citrus fruit. If you need only a little grated zest, use a hand grater. If you need a lot, remove the zest in strips with a zester or a vegetable peeler and pulverize it in a spice mill. Be sure not to include any of the bitter white pith when you remove the zest. Grated citrus zest is one of my favorite flavorings. It will keep in the refrigerator for up to a week.

VANILLA BEAN: Fresh vanilla bean has a much more intense flavor than vanilla extract. I recommend using a 2-inch piece, which you cut in half lengthwise. For maximum flavor, leave the vanilla bean in the cream or sauce until just before serving. When using vanilla extract, add it to warm, not hot, mixtures.

A FEW FINAL OBSERVATIONS

Unless otherwise stated, cakes and pastries should be baked in the lower third of the oven.

When scalding or boiling skim milk, stir it steadily with a wooden spoon, as its lack of fat makes it scorch more easily than whole milk.

While some of the recipes in this book contain no fat, most are low-fat. As readers of my previous books know, the philosophy I espouse is low-fat, not no-fat, cooking. I'd rather use a little fat to make great-tasting desserts than no fat to make food that tastes like medicine.

Finally, when a range of yields is given, the nutritional analysis is based on the lower yield.

Chocoholics Unanimous

Mega-Chocolate Roulade

This cake won the approval of the sternest critics, my wife and daughter, both of whom like their chocolate cakes loaded with butter, cream, and egg yolks. The secret is the filling, a chocolate pudding enriched with both cocoa powder and unsweetened chocolate.

Spray oil
½ cup cake flour, plus more for dusting
3 tablespoons unsweetened Dutch-processed cocoa powder
Pinch salt
½ cup plus 3 tablespoons granulated sugar

6 large egg whites
½ teaspoon cream of tartar
2 teaspoons vanilla extract
Intense Chocolate Pudding (see page 2)
Confectioners' sugar, for dusting

1. Make sure the rack is in the lower third of the oven and preheat the oven to 375° F. Line a 16 × 11-inch jelly-roll pan with baking parchment or foil, lightly spray it with oil, and dust with flour, shaking off the excess.

2. Sift the ½ cup flour, the cocoa, the salt, and the ½ cup sugar into a mixing bowl. Put the egg whites and cream of tartar in an electric mixer and beat to soft peaks, starting at slow speed, then increasing to medium, then to medium-high. When soft peaks form, add the remaining 3 tablespoons sugar and increase the speed to high. Continue beating until the whites are firm and glossy but not dry, about 30 seconds. (Beating will take about 6 to 8 minutes in all.) Stir in the vanilla. Sift the cocoa mixture into the egg whites in three batches, gently folding after each addition with a rubber spatula. Do not overmix. Spread the batter evenly in the prepared pan and gently tap the pan on the counter to knock out any air bubbles.

3. Bake the roulade until it feels firm and

springy to the touch, about 10 minutes. Remove the pan from the oven. Lift the roulade by the corners of the paper or foil and slide it onto a cake rack. Let cool to room temperature. Meanwhile, prepare the Intense Chocolate Pudding.

4. Assemble the roulade: Spread the cake with the chocolate pudding. Beginning at the wide end closer to you, gently roll up the cake, pulling the paper or foil to help you roll it.

When it is almost rolled up, transfer it, seam side down, to a long, narrow platter or foil-covered cardboard rectangle a little larger than the cake. The roulade can be prepared up to 3 hours ahead. Just before serving, dust the top with confectioners' sugar. To serve, cut it into ½- or 1-inch slices.   *Makes 1 16-inch roulade, which will serve 8 to 10*

204 CALORIES PER SERVING; 6 G PROTEIN; 3 G FAT; 10 G SATURATED FAT; 41 G CARBOHYDRATE; 109 MG SODIUM; 27 MG CHOLESTEROL

INTENSE CHOCOLATE PUDDING

This pudding began as a filling for a cake, but it was so rich, creamy, and intensely chocolaty that my family wound up eating it all by itself. It's very good made with basic supermarket chocolate and downright astonishing made with a designer chocolate like Valrhona.

8 tablespoons sugar, or to taste
3 tablespoons unsweetened Dutch-processed cocoa powder
1½ tablespoons cornstarch
1 large egg
1 cup skim or 1-percent milk

2-inch piece vanilla bean, split, or
    2 teaspoons vanilla extract
1 ounce unsweetened chocolate, finely chopped
Meringue Whipped Cream, for garnish (optional) (see page 5)

1. Put 5 tablespoons of the sugar, the cocoa, and the cornstarch in a mixing bowl and whisk to combine. Add the egg and whisk to mix. Put

the milk, the vanilla bean, and the remaining 3 tablespoons sugar in a heavy saucepan and bring to a boil, whisking often to keep the milk from scorching. (If you are using vanilla extract, wait until later to add—see step 3.)

2. Add the scalded milk to the egg mixture in a thin stream, whisking steadily. Return the mixture to the saucepan and bring to a boil, whisking steadily. Reduce the heat so that the mixture bubbles gently and cook until thickened, about 2 minutes.

3. Off the heat, stir in the chopped chocolate. (If you are using vanilla extract, add it now.) Taste and add more sugar if desired. Let the pudding cool to room temperature and refrigerate until serving. Remove the vanilla bean. To serve, spoon the pudding into martini glasses or wineglasses. If desired, garnish with dollops of Meringue Whipped Cream.

Makes 1 ½ cups, which will serve 2

329 CALORIES PER SERVING; 9 G PROTEIN; 9 G FAT; 4 G SATURATED FAT; 61 G CARBOHYDRATE; 89 MG SODIUM; 96 MG CHOLESTEROL

CHOCOLATE SILK PIE

Silk pie is an American classic, but most versions contain an unconscionable amount of butter. The meringue crust gives this one plenty of crunch without the fat. For a splurge, you could serve it with Meringue Whipped Cream (recipe follows).

Spray oil
12 chocolate wafer cookies
  (about ¼ cup cookie crumbs)
⅔ cup sugar
3 tablespoons unsweetened Dutch-processed
  cocoa powder

3 large egg whites
¼ teaspoon cream of tartar
1 teaspoon vanilla extract
Intense Chocolate Pudding (see page 2)
Meringue Whipped Cream (optional)
  (recipe follows)

1. Preheat the oven to 300° F. Lightly spray a 9-inch pie pan with oil. Grind the cookies to a powder in a food processor. Sprinkle with half the cookie crumbs and set aside. Stir together ⅓ cup of the sugar and the cocoa, and set aside.

2. Beat the egg whites in an electric mixer at low speed 1 minute. Add the cream of tartar. Gradually increase the speed and beat the whites to soft peaks. Add the remaining ⅓ cup sugar in a thin stream and continue beating until the whites are firm and glossy but not dry. Stir in the vanilla. Using a rubber spatula, fold in the cocoa mixture as gently as possible. Spoon the meringue into the crumb-lined pie pan, spreading it across the bottom and up the sides.

3. Bake the meringue until crisp, 1½ to 2 hours. Transfer the pan to a wire rack to cool. Meanwhile, prepare the Intense Chocolate Pudding.

4. Spoon the cooled pudding into the meringue shell and sprinkle with the remaining cookie crumbs. Cut into 8 wedges and serve with Meringue Whipped Cream, if desired.

Makes 1 9-inch pie, which will serve 8

337 CALORIES PER SERVING; 6 G PROTEIN; 11 G FAT; 2.7 G SATURATED FAT; 59 G CARBOHYDRATE; 205 MG SODIUM; 39 MG CHOLESTEROL

MERINGUE WHIPPED CREAM

Lightened with meringue, this whipped topping contains a fraction of the fat found in regular whipped cream.
For the best results in whipping the cream, chill the bowl, beaters, and cream in the freezer 20 minutes.

3 large egg whites
¼ teaspoon cream of tartar
½ cup plus 1 tablespoon sugar

3 tablespoons water
1 teaspoon vanilla extract
½ to ¾ cup heavy cream

1. Put the egg whites and cream of tartar in an electric mixer and start beating at low speed. Gradually increase the speed to medium and continue beating while you prepare the sugar syrup.

2. Put the ½ cup sugar and the water in a heavy saucepan with a lid. Cover and bring to a boil. Uncover and cook the sugar until medium-hot, to the softball stage (239° F. on a candy thermometer).

3. Increase the mixer speed to high and beat the whites to soft peaks. Add the remaining 1 tablespoon sugar and beat until the whites are glossy and firm but not dry. The process should take 8 minutes altogether. With the mixer running, pour the hot sugar syrup into the egg whites. Add the vanilla and continue beating until completely cool.

4. Using a clean bowl and beaters, beat the cream almost until stiff peaks form. Gently fold the meringue into the whipped cream with a rubber spatula.

Makes about 2 cups, which will serve 10 to 12

110 CALORIES PER SERVING; 2 G PROTEIN; 5.5 G FAT; 3.4 G SATURATED FAT; 14 G CARBOHYDRATE; 34 MG SODIUM; 20 MG CHOLESTEROL

CHOCOLATE MADELEINES

Madeleines are cake-like, shell-shaped cookies, of course, and they're so beloved by the French that a single bite was enough to inspire French novelist Marcel Proust to write Remembrance of Things Past. *We made lots of madeleines at the La Varenne cooking school in Paris, where the order of the day was "butter, butter, and more butter." Here's a low-fat chocolate madeleine created by my good friend Patsy Jamieson, a fellow La Varenner, who now runs the test kitchen at* Eating Well *magazine.*

Spray oil
1 cup unbleached all-purpose white flour,
    plus flour for dusting the mold
¼ cup unsweetened Dutch-processed cocoa
    powder
1½ teaspoons baking powder
½ teaspoon baking soda
½ cup low-fat buttermilk

2 tablespoons canola oil
1 tablespoon butter, melted
1 teaspoon vanilla extract
1 large egg, plus 1 large egg white
¾ cup sugar
¼ cup confectioners' sugar for sprinkling
Madeleine molds

1. Preheat the oven to 400° F. Spray the molds with oil and dust with flour, shaking out the excess. Combine the flour, cocoa, baking powder, and baking soda in a mixing bowl, whisk to mix, and set aside. Combine the buttermilk, oil, melted butter, and vanilla in another bowl and set aside.

2. Combine the egg, egg white, and sugar in an electric mixer. Beat until thick and foamy, starting on medium speed, then high, about 8 minutes in all. When the eggs are ready, the mixture will be pale-yellow and tripled in volume and will fall from a raised whisk in a thick, silky ribbon.

3. Sift the flour mixture into the egg mixture in three batches, alternately adding the buttermilk mixture and folding gently with a rubber spatula between each addition. Spoon the batter into the prepared molds, filling each ¾ of the way. Bake the madeleines until cooked, 12 to 15 minutes; when they are done, the tops will spring back when pressed lightly. Let the madeleines cool in the pans for 1 minute, then unmold onto a cake rack. Let cool completely.

Dust the madeleines (the ribbed side) with confectioners' sugar and serve.

Note: Madeleine molds are available at cookware shops. Or you can use small fluted tartlet molds.

Makes about 2 dozen

68 CALORIES PER PIECE; 1.3 G PROTEIN; 2 G FAT; 0.5 G SATURATED FAT; 12 G CARBOHYDRATE; 51 MG SODIUM; 10 MG CHOLESTEROL

COCOA KISSES

I've always loved hard meringues—the kind that make a deafening crunch when you bite into them. They gave me the idea for a low-fat "kiss": a teardrop of meringue that could be dipped in chocolate for extra richness. (The kisses are plenty delicious without it.) For truly crisp meringues, I like to bake them at a very low temperature and allow them to dry out in the oven's residual heat overnight.

Spray oil
Flour for dusting
⅔ cup sugar
3 tablespoons unsweetened Dutch-processed
   cocoa powder
½ teaspoon ground cinnamon (optional)
1 tablespoon cornstarch

3 large egg whites
¼ teaspoon cream of tartar
1 teaspoon vanilla extract
1 to 2 ounces semisweet or bittersweet
   chocolate (preferably Valrhona)
   (optional)

1. Preheat the oven to 200° F. Line a baking sheet with baking parchment. Lightly spray it with oil and dust with flour, shaking off the excess.

2. Sift ⅓ cup of the sugar and the cocoa, cinnamon, and cornstarch into a small bowl, and set aside. Beat the egg whites in an electric mixer at low speed 1 minute. Add the cream of tartar. Gradually increase the speed and beat the whites to soft peaks, about 6 to 8 minutes. Add the remaining ⅓ cup sugar in a thin stream and continue beating until the whites are firm and glossy but not dry. Stir in the vanilla. Using a rubber spatula, gently fold the cocoa mixture into the beaten whites.

3. Transfer the meringue to a pastry bag fitted with a ½-inch round or star tip. (A star tip will give you a ridged kiss.) Holding the tip ¼ inch above the baking sheet, pipe a 1-inch-wide ball, reducing the pressure and lifting the tip to taper it to a point. (You should wind up with a shape like a Hershey's kiss.) Repeat the process with the rest of the meringue.

4. Bake the meringues until they are firm and crisp, 3 to 4 hours. Turn off the heat and leave the meringues to dry out in the oven overnight. Gently pry the meringues off the baking sheet with a spatula.

5. If dipping the kisses, melt the chocolate in a bowl set over a pan of barely simmering water.

(Do not let even a drop of water come in contact with the chocolate, or it may "seize.") Holding a meringue by its base, dip it in the melted chocolate and let the excess drip off. Invert it onto a sheet of wax paper or parchment and let cool. Repeat the process with the other kisses. When they are completely cool, store them in an airtight container away from heat and light.   *Makes 5 to 6 dozen kisses*

10 CALORIES PER SERVING (1 KISS); 0.2 G PROTEIN; 0 G FAT; 0 G SATURATED FAT; 2.5 G CARBOHYDRATE; 4 MG SODIUM; 0 MG CHOLESTEROL

CAKES

BERRY SPONGECAKE WITH ORANGE CURD

Easy to make and impressive to serve, this summery cake has something for everyone. The recipe may seem involved, but actually it can be completed in less than an hour. For a great presentation, bake the cake in a "flan" pan— a cake pan with fluted sloping sides and a depression in the center (see photograph on page 10).

Basic Spongecake (recipe follows)
Orange Curd (see Note, page 56)

FOR THE GLAZE:
3 tablespoons apricot jam
2 to 3 tablespoons water (enough to thin the jam to brushable consistency)

TO ASSEMBLE THE CAKE:
1 pint fresh raspberries
1 pint fresh blackberries
1 quart strawberries, hulled

1. Prepare the spongecake and let cool. Prepare the orange curd and let cool.

2. Make the glaze: Put the jam and water in a small heavy saucepan and cook over medium heat, whisking steadily, until the jam is melted and syrupy, about 3 minutes.

3. Assemble the cake: Spoon the orange curd into the depression in the top of the cake. Arrange the berries on the top of the cake in concentric circles, alternating colors. Brush the berries with the apricot glaze. The cake can be prepared several hours ahead.

Makes 1 11-inch cake, which will serve 8 to 10

327 CALORIES PER SERVING; 7 G PROTEIN; 6 G FAT; 2.6 G SATURATED FAT; 65 G CARBOHYDRATE; 71 MG SODIUM; 88 MG CHOLESTEROL

BASIC SPONGECAKE

When recrafting traditional recipes for High-Flavor, Low-Fat cooking, I aim for results that equal the original. Sometimes I get lucky and the low-fat version actually tastes better. Such is the case with the following spongecake, my remake of a French génoise, in which I replaced half the egg yolks in the traditional recipe with whites. The result is an airy cake that's incredibly soft and velvety. (It also lacks the "eggy" taste of a génoise, which I find heavy.) The butter is browned to give it extra flavor, so you only need half as much as for a traditional génoise. I like to bake this cake in a "flan" pan—a cake pan with fluted sides and a depressed center—but you can use a standard round cake pan, too.

Spray oil
Dry bread crumbs or flour for dusting
1 cup cake flour
2 to 3 tablespoons unsalted butter
2 large eggs plus 4 large egg whites

⅔ cup sugar
2 teaspoons vanilla extract or orange-flower
   water (see page 18)
2 teaspoons grated lemon or orange zest

1. Preheat the oven to 350° F. Lightly spray an 11-inch flan pan or 9-inch round cake pan (preferably nonstick) with spray oil and place it in the freezer for 5 minutes. Line the bottom of the pan with baking parchment. (If using a flan pan, line only the flat central portion.) Spray the pan with oil again and place it in the freezer for 5 minutes. Sprinkle the pan with bread crumbs and tap it upside down to remove the excess.

2. Sift the flour into a small bowl. Melt the butter in a heavy saucepan set over medium-high heat and continue cooking it until it turns hazelnut brown. Immediately remove from the heat.

3. Put the eggs and sugar in an electric mixer and beat at low speed, gradually increasing to medium, then high. Beat 8 to 10 minutes in all, until the mixture is pale yellow and has tripled in volume, and falls from a raised whisk in a thick, silky ribbon. Stir in the vanilla and zest.

4. Sift the sifted flour onto the egg mixture in three batches, gently folding with a rubber spatula after each addition. Whisk about ½ cup of the batter into the melted butter. Return this mixture to the mixing bowl and fold just to combine. It's important to fold gently and just enough to combine: excess folding will deflate the eggs.

5. Spoon the batter into the prepared pan

and bake until the top of the cake feels firm and the sides start to pull away from the pan, and an inserted cake tester comes out clean, about 20 minutes. Remove the pan from the oven and let cool slightly. Invert the cake onto a wire rack and gently tap the pan to unmold it. Let the cake cool to room temperature.

Makes 1 11-inch cake with a depressed center or 1 regular 9-inch cake, which will serve 8 to 10

178 CALORIES PER SERVING; 5 G PROTEIN; 5 G FAT; 2.3 G SATURATED FAT; 29 G CARBOHYDRATE; 61 MG SODIUM; 62 MG CHOLESTEROL

LEMON POPPY CHIFFON CAKE

Chiffon cake might be thought of as angel food that's graduated from finishing school. The addition of oil gives chiffon cake extra refinement and moistness. Chiffon cakes are easy to make, but to be successful you must avoid the three don'ts. Don't overbeat the egg whites (they should be firm and glossy, but not dry). Don't overfold the batter (or you'll deflate it). And don't overbake the cake (or it will collapse).

½ cup canola oil
1 cup sugar, plus 3 tablespoons for the
   egg whites
½ cup fresh lemon juice (3 to 4 lemons)
1 tablespoon grated lemon zest
Pinch salt

¼ cup poppy seeds
1½ cups cake flour
1 tablespoon baking powder
8 egg whites (1 cup)
1 teaspoon cream of tartar
Lemon Glaze (optional) (recipe follows)

1. Preheat the oven to 325° F. Combine the oil, 1 cup sugar, lemon juice, lemon zest, salt, and poppy seeds in a mixing bowl and whisk to mix. Sift in the flour and baking powder and whisk just to mix.

2. Beat the egg whites in an electric mixer at slow speed for 1 minute. Add the cream of tartar and beat for 1 minute. Gradually increase the speed to medium, then medium-high, beating the egg whites to soft peaks. Increase the speed to high, beat in the remaining 3 tablespoons sugar, and beat until the whites are firm and glossy but not dry, about 30 seconds. The whole process should take 6 to 8 minutes. Do not overbeat. If you're not sure when the whites are done, err on the side of underbeating.

3. Gently stir ¼ of the whites into the flour mixture to lighten it. Fold this mixture as gently as possible into the remaining whites, using a rubber spatula. Fold as gently and as little as possible, just to mix. Pour the mixture into a 9-inch tube or bundt pan (preferably nonstick) that has been sprayed with oil and lightly floured and smooth the top with a spatula. Lightly tap the pan on the work surface to knock out any bubbles.

4. Bake the chiffon cake until the top feels firm and an inserted cake tester comes out clean, 30 to 40 minutes. Do not overbake. Remove the pan from the oven, invert it onto a raised wire rack or wine bottle, and let it cool completely, upside down. Gently loosen the

cake from the sides of the pan with the tip of a paring knife. Invert it onto a platter and give it a little shake: the cake should slide right out. If you like, drizzle the top with Lemon Glaze (recipe follows).

Makes 1 9-inch cake, which will serve 10 to 12

258 CALORIES PER SERVING; 4 G PROTEIN; 12.7 G FAT; 1 G SATURATED FAT; 35 G CARBOHYDRATE; 188 MG SODIUM; 0 MG CHOLESTEROL

LEMON GLAZE

1 cup confectioners' sugar

About 1½ tablespoons fresh lemon juice

Put the confectioners' sugar in a small bowl and whisk in enough lemon juice to obtain a thick glaze. Spoon the glaze over the cake and let harden before slicing the cake.

SCARLET ANGEL

When I set out to write this book, there was one cake that needed no tinkering with to reduce the fat: classic American angel food. Saffron may seem like an odd flavoring for such a cake, but there is a precedent for it in the Pennsylvania Dutch cake called Schwenkfelder. When buying saffron, look for it in thread form in small tubes or envelopes, as powdered saffron is rarely as flavorful.

½ teaspoon saffron threads
1 tablespoon warm water
1 cup sifted cake flour (see Note)
1½ cups granulated sugar (preferably superfine), sifted

¼ teaspoon salt
12 large egg whites (1½ cups)
1½ teaspoons cream of tartar
Confectioners' sugar for garnish

1. Preheat the oven to 350° F. Place the saffron threads in a small bowl and crush to a powder with the end of a wooden spoon. Add the water and let stand 5 minutes. Sift the sifted flour, ½ cup of the sifted granulated sugar, and the salt into a small mixing bowl.

2. Beat the egg whites in an electric mixer at slow speed 1 minute. Add the cream of tartar and continue beating until the mixture is frothy. Increase the speed to medium, then to medium-high, and beat the egg whites to soft peaks. The entire process should take 6 to 8 minutes. Increase the speed to high and add the remaining 1 cup granulated sugar in a thin stream. Add the saffron with its liquid and continue beating until the whites are glossy and firm but not dry, about 30 seconds. Do not over-

beat; it is better to err on the side of underbeating. Sift the flour mixture onto the beaten whites in three batches, gently folding with a rubber spatula after each addition.

3. Pour the batter into an ungreased 10-inch tube pan with a removable bottom and bake 45 minutes without opening the oven door. Test for doneness by gently pressing the top of the cake with your finger: it should feel firm to the touch and spring back when you lift your finger. If necessary, bake the cake a few minutes longer.

4. Remove the cake from the oven and invert onto its legs to cool. (If your pan doesn't have legs, invert it onto the neck of a bottle.) It's important to let the cake cool completely in an inverted position.

5. To unmold the cake, run a sharp knife

around the inside of the pan and around the tube, working as gently as possible. Unmold the cake onto a platter. (You may need to give it a gentle shake.) Just before serving, dust the cake with confectioners' sugar. Cut with a cake comb or a serrated knife.

Note: To measure sifted flour, place a measuring cup on a sheet of wax paper. Sift in flour to the desired level. Return spilled flour to its container.   *Makes 1 10-inch tube cake, which will serve 10 to 12*

176 CALORIES PER SERVING; 5 G PROTEIN; 0 G FAT; 40 G CARBOHYDRATE; 155 MG SODIUM; 0 MG CHOLESTEROL

BANANA CREAM ROULADE

Here's a feather-light, drop-dead-gorgeous roulade that will drive people bananas. You'll need one special ingredient—orange-flower water, which is available at Middle Eastern markets and gourmet shops. The perfumy sweetness of this ingredient reinforces the sweetness of the bananas. Grand Marnier makes an adequate though different-flavored substitute. Try to use apple bananas, which are short, stubby fruit with a perfumed apple flavor. My thanks to baking authority Flo Braker, who generously shared her recipe for this fat-free roulade, which is a sort of rolled angel food cake.

Spray oil
½ cup cake flour, plus more for dusting
9 tablespoons sugar
5 large egg whites (⅔ cup)

½ teaspoon cream of tartar
1 tablespoon orange-flower water
Pastry cream (recipe follows)
2 ripe bananas

1. Make sure the oven rack is in the lower third of the oven and preheat the oven to 375° F. Line a 16 × 11-inch jelly-roll pan with baking parchment or foil. Lightly spray it with spray oil and dust with flour, shaking off the excess.

2. Sift the ½ cup flour and 6 tablespoons of the sugar into a small bowl and set aside. Put the egg whites and cream of tartar in an electric mixer and beat to soft peaks, starting at slow speed and increasing to medium, then medium-high. Add the remaining 3 tablespoons sugar and increase the speed to high. Continue beating until the whites are firm and glossy but not dry, about 30 seconds. The entire process should take 6 to 8 minutes. Stir in the orange-flower water. Sift the flour mixture onto the egg whites in three batches, gently folding after each addition with a rubber spatula just to combine.

3. Spread the batter evenly in the prepared pan. Tap the pan on the counter to knock out any air bubbles. Bake until the roulade feels firm and springy, about 10 minutes. Lift the corners of the paper and slide the roulade onto a wire rack. Let cool to room temperature. Meanwhile, make the Pastry Cream.

4. Assemble the roulade: Thinly slice the bananas. Spread the cake with the pastry cream and arrange the sliced bananas on top. Beginning at the wide end closer to you, gently roll up the cake, pulling on the paper to help you roll it. When it is almost rolled up, invert the roulade onto a platter or foil-covered piece of cardboard a little larger than the cake. The roulade can be prepared up to 3 hours ahead. To serve, cut into ½-inch slices.

Makes 1 16-inch roulade, which will serve 8 to 10

Pastry Cream

The pastry cream I learned to prepare in Paris was dizzyingly rich with egg yolks. The following recipe is a perfect example of the High-Flavor, Low-Fat method: it contains only one egg, but the cinnamon stick, vanilla bean, and lemon and orange zest provide all the flavor you could wish for.

1 cup skim milk
1 cinnamon stick
2-inch piece vanilla bean, split
3 strips orange zest

3 strips lemon zest
4 tablespoons sugar
1½ tablespoons cornstarch
1 large egg

1. Put the milk, cinnamon, vanilla, orange zest, lemon zest, and 1 tablespoon of the sugar in a small nonreactive saucepan and gradually bring to a boil, stirring often to prevent the milk from scorching. Meanwhile, put the remaining 3 tablespoons sugar, the cornstarch, and the egg in a mixing bowl and whisk to combine.

2. Add the scalded milk to the egg mixture in a thin stream and whisk to mix. Return the mixture to the saucepan and bring to a boil, whisking steadily. Reduce the heat until the mixture bubbles gently and cook until thickened, about 2 minutes. Force the pastry cream through a strainer into a small bowl, pressing with a rubber spatula. Cover the bowl with plastic wrap, pressing it on top of the pastry cream to prevent a skin from forming. Make a slit in the plastic to allow the steam to escape. Let cool to room temperature before refrigerating.

Makes 1 cup

48 CALORIES PER SERVING; 2 G PROTEIN; 0.7 G FAT; 0.2 G SATURATED FAT; 9 G CARBOHYDRATE; 24 MG SODIUM; 27 MG CHOLESTEROL

PIES AND CHEESECAKE

N.C. (NUTRITIONALLY CORRECT) CHEESECAKE

Here's a reduced-fat cheesecake that's everything you want a cheesecake to be: tart, rich, creamy, and cheesy. Note: At 12 grams of fat per serving, it's on the higher end of the register. You could lower the fat dramatically by using no-fat cottage cheese and cream cheese, but the cheesecake won't be nearly so good. I believe that the occasional splurge can be as good for you as a generally steady low-fat diet.

Spray oil
1 pound low-fat (1-percent) cottage cheese
1 pound low-fat cream cheese, at room
   temperature
1¼ cups sugar
2 large eggs plus 4 large egg whites
   (or 1 cup egg substitute)

¼ cup fresh lemon juice
1 tablespoon grated lemon zest
Pinch salt
1 tablespoon vanilla extract
Mango sauce or blackberry sauce
   (optional) (see page 37)

1. Preheat the oven to 350° F. (The rack should be set in the lower third of the oven.) Bring 1 quart water to a boil. Wrap a piece of foil around the bottom and sides of an 8-inch springform pan. (This prevents water from leaking in.) Lightly spray the pan with spray oil.

2. Purée the cottage cheese in the food processor, scraping down the sides. This will take 2 to 3 minutes. Add the cream cheese and purée until smooth. Add the sugar and purée. Add the eggs, egg whites, lemon juice, lemon zest, and salt, and purée. Pour the mixture into the prepared pan. Tap the pan a few times on the work counter to knock out any bubbles.

3. Set the pan in a roasting pan in the oven. Add 1 inch boiling water to the pan and bake

the cheesecake until set, 40 to 50 minutes. To test for doneness, gently poke the side—when the top no longer jiggles, the cheesecake is cooked. Another test: an inserted cake tester will come out clean when the cheesecake is cooked. Do not overcook or the cheesecake will become watery.

4. Transfer the cheesecake to a wire rack to cool to room temperature, then refrigerate until cold. To serve, run the tip of a small knife around the inside of the pan. Unfasten the sides. If serving the cheesecake with the mango sauce or berry sauce, spoon it on top.

Note: To make a ginger cheesecake, add 1 tablespoon grated fresh ginger and 2 tablespoons finely chopped candied ginger after the vanilla and mask the sides of the cheesecake with gingersnap crumbs.

Makes 1 8-inch cheesecake,
which will serve 8 to 10

309 CALORIES PER SERVING; 16 G PROTEIN; 12 G FAT; 13 G SATURATED FAT; 37 G CARBOHYDRATE; 593 MG SODIUM; 76 MG CHOLESTEROL

Key Lime Pie

Key lime pie is one of the world's most refreshing desserts. I'm especially partial to it: it's the official dessert of my home state! The key lime is a small yellow fruit with a flavor that is both sour and bitter. To achieve a similar taste with widely available Persian limes, I add grated lime zest to both the filling and topping.

FOR THE CRUST:
1½ cups cinnamon-graham-cracker crumbs
  (about 15 square crackers)
2 tablespoons sugar
1 tablespoon butter, melted
2 tablespoons canola oil
1 large egg white, lightly beaten with a fork

FOR THE FILLING:
10 tablespoons fresh lime juice (4 to 6 limes)
1 tablespoon grated lime zest
2 tablespoons cornstarch

1 (14-ounce) can nonfat sweetened
  condensed skim milk
2 eggs

FOR THE MERINGUE:
4 egg whites
½ teaspoon cream of tartar
¾ cup sugar
3 tablespoons water
1 teaspoon grated lime zest
Spray oil

1. Preheat the oven to 350° F. Lightly spray a 9-inch tart pan with removable sides (preferably nonstick) with spray oil.

2. Make the crust: Put the graham-cracker crumbs, sugar, butter, oil, and egg white in a mixing bowl and combine with your fingers or a fork until moist and crumbly. (Alternatively, you can use a food processor.) Press the crumb mixture into the bottom and sides of the pie pan, using the back of a large spoon to smooth it. Bake until the crust is firm and lightly browned, about 10 minutes. Let cool to room temperature. Leave oven on.

3. While the crust is baking, prepare the filling. Put the lime juice, zest, cornstarch, condensed milk, and eggs in a heavy saucepan and whisk until smooth, about 2 minutes. Bring the filling to a boil, whisking steadily; it will thicken. Remove the pan from the heat and let the filling cool to room temperature. Spoon it into the crust.

4. Prepare the meringue: Place the egg

whites in an electric mixer and start beating at low speed, about 1 minute. Add the cream of tartar. Gradually increase the speed to medium and continue beating until frothy, about 30 seconds. Keep the mixer at medium while you cook the sugar.

5. Place ½ cup of the sugar and the water in a saucepan with a lid. Cover and bring to a boil. Uncover and cook over medium-high heat to the softball stage (239° F. on a candy thermometer).

6. When the cooked sugar is ready, increase the mixer speed to high and beat the whites to soft peaks. Add the remaining ¼ cup sugar and beat until the whites are glossy and firm but not dry. The whole process will take about 8 minutes. With the mixer running, pour the hot sugar mixture and 1 teaspoon lime zest into the egg whites and continue beating until cool.

7. Adjust the broiler rack so that it is 6 inches below the heating element and preheat the broiler. (If your rack cannot be lowered sufficiently, bake at 500° F. for 5 to 8 minutes.) Spread or pipe the meringue in decorative swirls or rosettes on top of the filling. Run the pie under the broiler to brown the meringue, 1 to 2 minutes. Watch carefully, because the meringue burns easily. Refrigerate until serving.

Makes 1 9-inch pie, which will serve 8

373 CALORIES PER SERVING; 9 G PROTEIN; 8 G FAT; 1.8 G SATURATED FAT; 68 G CARBOHYDRATE; 205 MG SODIUM; 62 MG CHOLESTEROL

SWEET-POTATO PIE

Silky-smooth and spicy is this sweet-potato pie, a healthy remake of a Southern classic. High-heat roasting caramelizes the sugars in the sweet potatoes, producing a firm, dense consistency and exceptionally rich flavor. I've called for one whole egg in the filling, but you could further reduce the fat by using all whites (you'd need 6 in all or ⅔ cup egg substitute).

1½ pounds sweet potatoes (3 to 4 potatoes,
   2 cups pulp)
¾ cup packed dark-brown sugar
1 large egg plus 4 large egg whites or
   ¾ cup egg substitute
1 cup evaporated skim milk
1 teaspoon ground cinnamon
½ teaspoon ground ginger

⅛ teaspoon ground cloves
⅛ teaspoon grated nutmeg (3 passes
   on a grater)
2 tablespoons dark rum
1 teaspoon vanilla extract
9-inch prebaked Reduced-Fat Pie Shell
   (see page 26)

1. Preheat the oven to 400° F. Scrub the sweet potatoes and put them in a baking dish. Roast until very soft, about 40 minutes. Remove the pan from the oven and reduce the heat to 350° F. (You can roast the sweet potatoes up to 2 days ahead.) When the sweet potatoes are cool enough to handle, peel them and purée the flesh in a food processor. (Alternatively, you can mash them with a potato masher and stir in the remaining ingredients by hand.) You should have 2 cups.

2. Add the sugar and the eggs or egg substitute and process until smooth. Add the milk, cinnamon, ginger, cloves, nutmeg, rum, and vanilla, and process to mix. Spoon the filling into the pie shell.

3. Bake until the filling is set, 20 to 30 minutes. Transfer to a wire rack to cool. Cut into 8 or 10 wedges to serve.

Makes 1 9-inch pie, which will serve 8 to 10

371 CALORIES PER SERVING; 9 G PROTEIN; 9 G FAT; 3.2 SATURATED FAT; 62 G CARBOHYDRATE; 273 MG SODIUM; 39 MG CHOLESTEROL

REDUCED-FAT PIE SHELL

*There's no way to make a crisp, flaky pie shell completely without fat. In the following recipe, I've replaced some
of the butter with canola oil, which is a more healthful type of fat. The cornmeal and cake flour
make the crust a little more crumbly than straight all-purpose flour would.*

¾ cup unbleached all-purpose white flour
  (plus more as needed)
3 tablespoons cake flour
3 tablespoons fine cornmeal
½ teaspoon salt
2½ tablespoons cold unsalted butter (if using
  salted butter, reduce the salt above to
  ¼ teaspoon)

1 egg white
1½ tablespoons canola oil
3 tablespoons ice water, or as needed

1. Place the all-purpose flour, cake flour, cornmeal, salt, and butter in a food processor fitted with a chopping blade. Run the machine to cut in the butter: the mixture should feel crumbly, like sand.

2. Add the egg white, oil, and ice water. Pulse until the dough comes together into a smooth ball. (If the mixture looks too dry, add a little more ice water.) Flatten the ball of dough into a disk, wrap in plastic and refrigerate until firm, about 1 hour.

3. Preheat the oven to 400° F. Roll out the dough into an 11-inch circle on a lightly floured work surface, flouring the rolling pin as well. You can also roll it between 2 sheets of plastic

wrap. Use the dough circle to line a 9-inch pie pan. Crimp or pleat the edges with your fingers or a fork. Prick the bottom of the crust with a fork and line with a sheet of foil. Freeze the crust for 5 minutes.

4. Fill the foil-lined crust with beans or rice and bake for 15 minutes. (The beans/rice hold the crust in shape during cooking.) Remove the beans or rice and foil and continue baking the crust until golden brown on the sides and bottom, 5 to 10 minutes more. Remove the crust from the oven and let it cool to room temperature before filling.

Makes 1 9-inch pie shell, enough to serve 8 to 10

RHUBARB MERINGUE TARTLETS

These tangy tartlets feature the world's easiest-to-make low-fat shells, made from eggroll wrappers.

FOR THE SHELLS:
Spray oil or 1½ tablespoons butter, melted
6 eggroll wrappers

FOR THE FILLING:
1½ pounds fresh or frozen rhubarb, trimmed
   and sliced ½ inch thick

¼ cup sugar or honey, or to taste
¼ cup fresh apple cider or water
1 cinnamon stick
2 strips lemon zest
1 batch of meringue, see page 23

1. Preheat the oven to 400° F. Lightly spray 6 3½-inch tartlet molds (or a muffin tin) with spray oil or brush with melted butter. Line each pan with an eggroll wrapper, pushing the dough into the ridges on the sides and trimming the excess with scissors. Lightly spray the shells with oil or brush with butter. Bake until crisp and golden brown, 10 to 15 minutes. Remove the shells from the pans and transfer to a wire rack to cool.

2. Prepare the filling: Put the rhubarb, sugar, cider, cinnamon, and zest in a large heavy saucepan. Cook over medium heat, stirring occasionally, until the rhubarb is soft, 6 to 8 minutes. Taste and correct the sweetness with more sugar if necessary. Remove and discard the cinnamon stick and strips of zest. Let the mixture cool to room temperature, then refrigerate until cold.

3. Prepare the meringue, following the instructions on page 23. Preheat broiler or oven to 500° F. Assemble the tartlets: Divide the filling equally among the shells. Using a pastry bag, pipe swirls or rosettes of meringue on top. Put the tartlets under the broiler to brown the meringue, about 2 minutes, or bake in oven for 5 to 8 minutes. The components can be prepared ahead, but the tartlets taste best served within 1 hour of assembly.   *Makes 6 tartlets*

168 CALORIES PER TARTLET; 4 G PROTEIN; 3 G FAT; 1.8 G SATURATED FAT; 32 G CARBOHYDRATE; 73 MG SODIUM; 15 MG CHOLESTEROL

PASTRIES AND CREPES

APPLE TURNOVERS

I'll never forget my first "exam" at the La Varenne cooking school in Paris. I was asked to prepare chaussons aux pommes—apple turnovers. This required the laborious confection of puff pastry, a process that used more butter for a single dessert than I would now go through in a fortnight. My low-fat version features filo dough lightly brushed with a mixture of butter and oil and layered with bread crumbs and sugar for extra crunch. Leftover turnovers make a great treat for breakfast.

FOR THE FILLING:

2 pounds firm tart apples, peeled, cored, and
  cut into ¼-inch dice (about 5 cups)
3 tablespoons fresh lemon juice,
  plus more as needed
Grated zest of 1 lemon
2 cups apple cider
1 cinnamon stick
2-inch piece vanilla bean, split
⅛ teaspoon ground cloves
¼ cup packed light-brown sugar, or to taste
¾ cup raisins
1 tablespoon cornstarch

1 tablespoon dark rum
1 to 2 tablespoons lightly toasted bread
  crumbs

TO FINISH THE TURNOVERS:

Spray oil
1½ tablespoons butter, melted
1½ tablespoons light olive oil or canola oil
¼ cup lightly toasted bread crumbs or
  graham-cracker crumbs
¼ cup granulated sugar
12 14 × 18-inch sheets filo dough
Confectioners' sugar for dusting

1. For the filling: In a nonreactive bowl, toss the diced apple with the 3 tablespoons lemon juice to prevent discoloration. Put the zest, cider, cinnamon, vanilla, cloves, and brown sugar in a

large nonreactive saucepan and bring to a boil. Reduce the heat to medium, add the apples and raisins, and gently simmer until the apples are tender but not too soft, 3 to 5 minutes.

2. Remove the apples and raisins with a slotted spoon and reserve. Boil the liquid until it is reduced to a thick, syrupy glaze. Remove and discard the cinnamon stick and vanilla bean. Dissolve the cornstarch in the rum and stir the apple mixture into the glaze. Return the apples and raisins to the pot and bring to a boil: the mixture will thicken. Taste and correct the seasoning with brown sugar or lemon juice. Transfer the mixture to a bowl set over ice and stir until cold. The cooled mixture should be fairly dry; if it is too wet, add 1 to 2 tablespoons bread crumbs.

3. Preheat the oven to 400° F. Lightly spray a nonstick baking pan with spray oil. Finish the turnovers: Combine the melted butter and oil in one small bowl, the bread crumbs or graham-cracker crumbs and granulated sugar in another. Place the filo sheets on a work surface that has been covered with plastic wrap. Place a piece of plastic wrap on top of the filo and cover it with a damp dish towel. Keep the sheets of filo covered until the last possible moment to prevent them from drying out as you work.

4. Lay one sheet of filo dough on a cutting board with a short edge toward you. Lightly brush it with the butter mixture and sprinkle with 2 level teaspoonfuls of the bread-crumb mixture. Lay another sheet of filo on top of it, brush with the butter mixture, and sprinkle with a heaping teaspoonful of the bread-crumb mixture. Cut the sheet lengthwise into 3 strips.

5. Place 2 to 3 tablespoons of the apple mixture 2 inches below the top edge of each strip in the center. Fold a top corner of the strip over the filling, lining up the edges to form a triangle. Continue folding the strip (as you would a flag) to obtain a triangle-shaped turnover. Repeat the process with the other 2 strips, and then with the rest of the filo dough and filling, to make 18 turnovers. Lightly brush the tops of the turnovers with the butter mixture and transfer them to the prepared baking pan. (The turnovers can be frozen at this stage and thawed overnight in the refrigerator.)

6. Bake the turnovers until they are crisp and nicely browned, 15 to 20 minutes. Transfer them to a wire rack to cool slightly. Dust with confectioners' sugar and serve at once.

Makes 18 turnovers (2 to 3 per person)

251 CALORIES PER SERVING; 2 G PROTEIN; 5 G FAT; 1.6 G SATURATED FAT; 54 G CARBOHYDRATE; 84 MG SODIUM; 5 MG CHOLESTEROL

BANANA STRUDEL

Here's a tropical remake of a classic Austrian dessert. My favorite banana for this recipe is the apple banana, but any banana will do.

FOR THE FILLING:
5 large ripe bananas
½ cup raisins
Juice and grated zest of 1 lemon
1 cinnamon stick
2-inch piece vanilla bean, split
1 tablespoon dark rum
¼ cup packed light-brown sugar, or to taste
1 tablespoon cornstarch
1 tablespoon banana liqueur (or more rum)

TO FINISH THE STRUDEL:
1 tablespoon butter, melted
1 tablespoon light olive oil or canola oil
¼ cup cinnamon-graham-cracker crumbs or dry bread crumbs (plus extra for sprinkling)
¼ cup granulated sugar
8 14 × 18-inch sheets filo dough

1. For the filling: Thinly slice the bananas and put them in a heavy nonreactive saucepan. Add the raisins, lemon juice and zest, cinnamon, vanilla, rum, and brown sugar, and stir to combine. Cook over medium heat until the bananas are just tender, 2 to 4 minutes. Correct the sweetness with more brown sugar if necessary.

2. Stir the cornstarch into the banana liqueur and add it to the bananas. Simmer 30 seconds, or until the mixture thickens. Let the filling cool to room temperature and remove the cinnamon stick and vanilla bean. Refrigerate the filling until cold.

3. Preheat the oven to 375° F. Finish the strudel: Combine the melted butter and oil in one small bowl, the graham-cracker crumbs and sugar in another. Place the filo sheets on a work surface that has been covered with plastic wrap. Place a piece of plastic wrap on top of the filo and cover it with a damp dish towel. Keep the sheets of filo covered until the last possible moment to prevent them from drying out as you work.

4. Lay one sheet of filo dough on a clean dish towel with a long edge toward you. Lightly brush it with some of the butter mixture and sprinkle with a level tablespoon of the crumb

mixture. Lay another sheet of filo on top, brush with more of the butter mixture, and sprinkle with the crumb mixture. Repeat with a third and fourth sheet of filo.

5. Mound half the banana filling in a row along the long edge closer to you. Roll up halfway, lifting the dish towel to help. Fold in the short ends and continue rolling the strudel. Carefully transfer it, seam side down, to a baking sheet. Assemble the second strudel the same way. Brush the tops of the strudels with the rest of the butter mixture and sprinkle with the rest of the crumb mixture.

6. Using a sharp knife, lightly score the tops of the strudels (don't cut all the way through to the filling). Bake the strudels until they are crisp and golden brown, 30 to 40 minutes. Let cool slightly, then cut into slices on the diagonal with a serrated knife.

Note: You could also spoon the banana filling into the Filo Nests on page 33.

Makes 2 strudels, which will serve 8 to 10

218 CALORIES PER SERVING; 2 G PROTEIN; 4 G FAT; 1.3 G SATURATED FAT; 46 G CARBOHYDRATE; 61 MG SODIUM; 4 MG CHOLESTEROL

FILO NESTS

Filo Nests are the easiest of all filo-dough confections to make, yet these freeform pastry shells with their delicately crinkled sides make for a dramatic presentation. Possible fillings include Lemon Curd or Orange Curd (see page 56), Intense Chocolate Pudding (see page 2), Duet of Poached Pears (see page 47), and Banana Strudel filling (see page 31).

4 14 × 18-inch sheets filo dough
Spray oil

1 tablespoon light olive oil or canola oil, or a mixture of the two

1. Preheat the oven to 400° F. Lightly spray 8 3½-inch tartlet molds or a muffin tin with spray oil. Place the filo sheets on a work surface that has been covered with plastic wrap. Place a piece of plastic wrap on top of the filo and cover it with a damp dish towel. Keep the sheets of filo covered until the last possible moment to prevent them from drying out as you work.

2. Lay one sheet of filo dough on a cutting board with a long edge toward you. Lightly brush it with the oil. Cut the sheet in half crosswise and then into 6 strips lengthwise, each about 2¼ inches wide. Use these 12 rectangles to line 2 of the tartlet molds. Tuck one end of the strip into a corner of a mold. Bring the remainder of the strip across the bottom, up the side, and into the air, crinkling it slightly as shown on page 46. Add a second strip at a 60-degree angle to the first and continue forming the sides of the nest. Continue lining the mold until 6 strips are used up. Line the other mold the same way, and repeat the process with the other sheets of filo dough and other molds.

3. Bake the Filo Nests until they are crisp and golden brown, about 10 minutes. Transfer to a wire rack to cool. Keep them in a cool, dry place. If they become soggy, recrisp them in a 350° F. oven. *Makes 8 Filo Nests*

25 CALORIES PER NEST; 0.5 G PROTEIN; 1 G FAT; 0.9 SATURATED FAT; 3 G CARBOHYDRATE; 30 MG SODIUM; 4 MG CHOLESTEROL

CREAM-FILLED CREPES

When I learned to make crepes at cooking school in Paris, my teachers would compete to see who could put the most butter and eggs in the batter. They'd probably be astonished by the following crepes, which are virtually fat-free. The trick is to replace most of the eggs with egg whites and use low-fat buttermilk in place of butter. Note: Be very careful when you flambé. Keep your face away from the pan and take care not to spill any of the flaming liquid on the tablecloth, the napkins, or your clothes.

FOR THE CREPES:
1 large egg plus 2 large egg whites
½ cup low-fat buttermilk
¾ cup water, plus more as necessary
½ teaspoon sugar
½ teaspoon salt, or to taste
1 teaspoon canola oil
1 cup unbleached white flour
Spray oil

FOR THE FILLING:
Lemon Curd (see page 56), Orange Curd (see Note, page 56), or Intense Chocolate Pudding (see page 2)

FOR THE FLAMBÉING (OPTIONAL):
½ cup rum (preferably 150—see Note)

1. Put the egg and the egg whites in a mixing bowl and whisk to combine. Whisk in the buttermilk, water, sugar, salt, and oil. Sift in the flour and whisk gently just to mix. (Do not overmix, or the crepes will be rubbery.) If the batter looks lumpy, strain it. It should be the consistency of heavy cream. If it is too thick, thin it with a little more water.

2. Lightly spray a 7-inch frying pan or crepe pan with oil and heat over a medium flame until a drop of water evaporates in 2 to 3 seconds. Off the heat, add a scant ¼ cup of crepe batter to the pan all at once. Gently tilt and rotate the pan to coat the bottom with a thin layer of batter. Pour back any excess; the crepe should be as thin as possible. Cook until the crepe is lightly browned on both sides, 1 to 2 minutes per side, turning it with a spatula. As the crepes are done, stack them on a plate. For the best results, spray the pan with oil after each one. The crepes can be prepared up to 24 hours ahead to this stage. Store in the refrigerator on a plate covered with plastic wrap.

3. Arrange a crepe, pale side up, on a plate. Place a heaping tablespoonful of filling in the center. Roll up the crepe or fold it in half, then

in half again. Arrange the crepes on individual plates or a large platter.

4. To flambé the crepes, gently warm the rum in a small saucepan, being careful not to let it boil or even become too hot to touch. Bring a lighted match to the surface of the rum and stand back: it will ignite. Pour the flaming rum over the crepes and serve at once.

Note: 150 rum is an overproof rum that's great for flambéing because it seems to burn forever, but regular rum or brandy will work, too.

Makes 14 to 16 crepes

112 CALORIES PER SERVING; 3 G PROTEIN; 1 G FAT; 0.3 G SATURATED FAT; 24 G CARBOHYDRATE; 103 MG SODIUM; 31 MG CHOLESTEROL

Meringues and Soufflés

Pistachio Floating Islands
with Mango and Berry Drizzle

Ile flottante (floating island) is one of the first desserts one learns to make at French cooking school. Nothing could be easier than this: a simple meringue baked in a nut-and-sugar-lined mold. In these individual-sized floating islands I've reduced the amount of nuts and replaced the traditional egg yolk–laden custard sauce with two colorful fruit sauces.

2 to 3 tablespoons shelled pistachio nuts, lightly toasted
3 tablespoons granulated sugar
Spray oil or 1½ tablespoons butter, melted

FOR THE MERINGUES:
5 large egg whites, at room temperature
½ teaspoon cream of tartar
1 cup granulated sugar
1 teaspoon grated lemon zest
1 teaspoon vanilla extract
½ teaspoon pistachio or almond extract

FOR THE MANGO SAUCE:
1 ripe mango (10 to 12 ounces)
2 tablespoons fresh lime juice, or to taste
2 tablespoons confectioners' sugar, or to taste
¼ cup fresh orange juice or water, plus more as needed

FOR THE BERRY SAUCE:
3 cups fresh or frozen blackberries or raspberries
⅓ cup confectioners' sugar, or to taste

1. Preheat the oven to 350° F. Put the pistachios and sugar in a food processor and grind to a coarse powder in bursts. (Be careful not to overgrind, or overprocess, or you'll reduce

Pistachio Floating Islands with Mango and Berry Drizzle

the mixture to an oily paste.) Spray 6 1-cup-capacity custard cups or coffee cups with rounded bottoms with spray oil and sprinkle with the pistachio mixture, shaking any excess into the next cup. Bring a kettle of water to a boil.

2. Make the meringues: Beat the egg whites in an electric mixer at low speed 1 minute. Add the cream of tartar. Gradually increase the speed to medium, then medium-high, and beat the whites to soft peaks. Add ¼ cup of the sugar in a thin stream and continue beating until the whites are firm and glossy but not dry. Using a rubber spatula, fold the remaining ¾ cup sugar, and the zest, vanilla, and pistachio extract into the whites as gently as possible. Spoon this mixture into the pistachio-lined cups. Set the cups in a roasting pan, place it in the oven, and add boiling water to 1 inch.

3. Bake the meringues 30 minutes, or until they are puffed and firm but not browned. (It's normal for the meringues to rise like a soufflé; they'll fall as they cool.) Remove the pan from the oven and let the meringues cool until they have fallen but are still warm. Invert them onto individual plates or a large platter: you may need to give the cup a little shake to ease out the meringue.

4. While the meringues are cooking, prepare the sauces: Peel the mango and cut the flesh off the seed. Purée the mango in a food processor with the lime juice and sugar. Add enough orange juice to obtain a pourable consistency and correct the flavoring with lime juice and sugar. Strain the sauce into a bowl: you should have about 1¼ cups.

5. Purée the berries with the sugar in a food processor, running the machine in bursts. (Be careful not to overprocess, or you'll crush the seeds and make the sauce bitter.) Correct the sweetness with more sugar if necessary. Strain the sauce into a bowl: you should have about ¾ cup.

6. Ladle a pool of mango sauce around the meringues. Place the berry sauce in a squirt bottle and make decorative squiggles on the sauce-free lip of the plate or platter.

Note: To make a completely fat-free dessert, eliminate the pistachio nuts and increase the amount of sugar used for lining the molds. If you are using frozen berries, measure the 3-cup amount while they are still hard, because they lose their shape and take up less room when they thaw. Defrost before puréeing.

Makes 6 Floating Islands

283 CALORIES PER FLOATING ISLAND; 5 G PROTEIN; 2 G FAT; 0.2 G SATURATED FAT; 66 G CARBOHYDRATE; 67 MG SODIUM; 0 MG CHOLESTEROL

NATILLAS WITH MULLED-CIDER SYRUP AND DRIED-FRUIT COMPOTE

Natillas are the Southwest's answer to the French dessert oeufs à la neige—*snowy poached meringue "eggs" drizzled with spice-scented cider syrup. The compote features two indigenous American foods, cranberries and blueberries. This recipe comes from my friend the Southwestern cuisine mogul Mark Miller.*

FOR THE CIDER SYRUP:
6 cups fresh apple cider
¾ cup sugar
3 tablespoons fresh lemon juice
4 strips lemon zest
2 cinnamon sticks
1 tablespoon allspice berries, lightly crushed
1 star anise
½ teaspoon whole cloves

FOR THE DRIED-FRUIT COMPOTE:
½ cup dried apricots, cut in half
½ cup dried pears, cut in half
½ cup dried cranberries
½ cup dried blueberries
½ cup dried cherries or raisins

FOR THE MERINGUES:
7 large egg whites
½ teaspoon cream of tartar
½ teaspoon ground cinnamon
1¼ cups sugar

1. Put the cider, sugar, lemon juice, zest, cinnamon sticks, allspice, star anise, and cloves in a large heavy nonreactive saucepan and bring to a boil. Reduce the heat and briskly simmer 3 minutes. Remove 2 cups of cider and reserve. Continue simmering the remaining cider until reduced to 2 cups. Strain this into a bowl and let cool.

2. Prepare the compote: Put the apricots, pears, cranberries, blueberries, and cherries in a medium saucepan and add the 2 cups reserved cider. Gently simmer, stirring gently, until the fruits are soft and most of the liquid has been absorbed, 5 to 10 minutes. Let the compote cool.

3. Make the meringues: Bring 1 inch of water to the barest simmer in a large frying pan. Beat the egg whites in an electric mixer at low speed 1 minute. Add the cream of tartar. Gradually increase the speed to medium, then

medium-high, and beat the whites to soft peaks. Add the cinnamon and then the sugar in a thin stream, and continue beating until the whites are firm and glossy but not dry.

4. Using two 2-inch soup spoons, form ovals of meringue and gently place them in the barely simmering water. Rinse the spoons with water between scoops to prevent sticking. Poach the meringues until slightly puffed and firm, 4 to 5 minutes on one side and 2 to 3 minutes on the other, turning them with a slotted spoon or a fork. (Take care not to crowd the pan and do not overcook, or the meringues will collapse.) Transfer the meringues with a slotted spoon to paper towels to drain. (It's normal for the meringues to deflate a little on cooling.)

5. To assemble the natillas, place a mound of fruit compote on each of 8 deep dessert plates or shallow bowls. Arrange the meringue eggs (2 or 3 per serving) around the compote, evenly spaced, one end touching or propped up on the compote. Drizzle 3 to 4 tablespoons of the cider syrup over the meringues and around the plate. Serve at once.

Note: Any dried fruits can be substituted for the ones listed here. You will need 2½ cups in all.

Serves 8

381 CALORIES PER SERVING; 5 G PROTEIN; 0.4 G FAT; 0 G SATURATED FAT; 98 G CARBOHYDRATE; 71 MG SODIUM; 0 MG CHOLESTEROL

PUDIM DE CLARAS (APRICOT-CARAMEL MERINGUE)

This dessert is a sort of Brazilian floating island. Any dried fruit could be substituted for the apricots.

1¾ cups sugar
¾ cup dried apricots
2 tablespoons finely chopped candied ginger

2 teaspoons grated lemon zest
6 large egg whites
½ teaspoon cream of tartar

1. Preheat the oven to 350° F. Sprinkle ¾ cup of the sugar in a deep, one-piece, 8-inch, 8-cup-capacity ring mold. Heat the mold directly on the burner over medium-low heat until the sugar melts into a golden-brown caramel, about 10 minutes, rotating the mold to ensure even melting and coating. Use a spoon to coat the tube section. Take care to avoid being burned by the hot caramel. Let cool.

2. Put the apricots in a small saucepan and add water to cover. Gently simmer the apricots until very tender, 6 to 8 minutes. Drain, reserving 3 tablespoons of the water. Purée the apricots with the reserved water in a food processor and stir in the candied ginger and lemon zest.

3. Beat the egg whites in an electric mixer at low speed 1 minute. Add the cream of tartar. Gradually increase the speed to medium, then medium-high, and beat the whites to soft peaks. Gradually add the remaining 1 cup sugar in a thin stream and continue beating until the whites are firm and glossy but not dry. Using a rubber spatula, gently fold the apricot purée into the egg whites. Spoon this mixture into the caramel-lined mold. Set the mold in a roasting pan, place it in the oven, and add boiling water to 1 inch.

4. Bake until the meringue is firm and puffed, about 40 minutes. Avoid opening the oven door. (It's normal for the meringue to rise like a soufflé; it will fall to the proper height as it cools.) Turn off the oven and let the meringue cool 1 hour without opening the oven door.

5. Run the tip of a knife around the inside of the mold. Place a platter over the mold and invert: the meringue should slide out easily. If not, give the mold a gentle shake. Spoon any caramel that remains in the mold on top of the meringue. Cut into wedges and serve.

Makes 6 to 8 servings

277 CALORIES PER SERVING; 4 G PROTEIN; 0 G FAT; 0 G SATURATED FAT; 69 G CARBOHYDRATE; 76 MG SODIUM; 0 MG CHOLESTEROL

TROPICAL FRUIT PAVLOVAS

Pavlova is New Zealand's national dessert: crisp meringue shells filled with whipped cream and fresh fruit. (The dish is named for the legendary dancer Anna Pavlova, who toured New Zealand in 1926.) The meringue shell makes a crisp counterpoint to the soft, ripe tropical fruits in this recipe. The traditional whipped cream has been replaced with a creamy blend of low-fat cream cheese, sour cream, and silken tofu.

FOR THE MERINGUES:
Spray oil
Flour for dusting
5 large egg whites
½ teaspoon cream of tartar
1 cup plus 2 tablespoons granulated sugar,
    preferably turbinado (see Note)
1 teaspoon vanilla extract

FOR THE LEMON CREAM:
5 tablespoons confectioners' sugar
3 ounces low-fat cream cheese

½ cup nonfat sour cream
2 ounces (4 tablespoons) silken tofu
    (see Note)
½ teaspoon grated lemon zest

TO ASSEMBLE THE PAVLOVAS:
4 cups diced mixed tropical fruits, such as
    mango, papaya, banana, pineapple,
    cherimoya, and star fruit—the star fruit
    should be sliced, not diced
2 teaspoons fresh lime juice
Mint sprigs, for garnish

1. The day before or early in the morning, prepare the meringues: Spray 1 large or 2 small baking sheets with oil and lightly dust with flour. Trace eight 3½-inch circles in the flour, using a ramekin or cup as a guide. Preheat the oven to 250° F.

2. Beat the egg whites in an electric mixer at low speed 1 minute. Add the cream of tartar. Gradually increase the speed to medium, then medium-high, and beat the whites to soft peaks.

Add ¼ cup of the sugar in a thin stream and continue beating until the whites are firm and glossy but not dry. As gently as possible, fold in the remaining ¾ cup plus 2 tablespoons sugar and the vanilla.

3. Transfer the meringue to a pastry bag fitted with a ½-inch round or star tip. Starting in the center and working outward, pipe circles of meringue onto the baking sheets, using the tracings as guides. Pipe a ring of meringue on

top of each circle at the outside edge to form a shallow bowl-shaped shell.

4. Bake the meringues until they are crisp and dry but not browned, 4 to 6 hours. Let them cool completely, then gently lift them off the baking sheet with a spatula. (The meringues can be prepared ahead and stored in an airtight container.)

5. Prepare the lemon cream: Put the confectioners' sugar, cream cheese, sour cream, tofu, and zest in a food processor and process to a smooth paste, scraping down the edges of the bowl with a rubber spatula.

6. Assemble the Pavlovas: Not more than 20 minutes before serving, spoon the lemon cream into the meringue shells. Toss the fruits with the lime juice to prevent them from browning. Spoon the fruits into the meringue shells. (It looks nice if you place a slice of star fruit on top of each mound.) Garnish with a mint sprig and serve at once.

Note: Turbinado is a granulated light-brown sugar available in most supermarkets. Silken tofu is a soft, creamy tofu available in natural foods stores, gourmet shops, Asian markets, and many supermarkets. One good brand is Mori Nu.

Makes 8 Pavlovas

247 CALORIES PER PAVLOVA; 6 G PROTEIN; 3 G FAT; 2.4 G SATURATED FAT; 54 G CARBOHYDRATE; 140 MG SODIUM; 4 MG CHOLESTEROL

FLAMING GRAND MARNIER AND CHOCOLATE CHUNK SOUFFLÉ

Soufflés are the ultimate indulgence. We make them often at our house—not only on account of their elegance, but for the fact that they require only 10 minutes of preparation time and can be made with ingredients you almost always have on hand. The one or two optional egg yolks in the following recipe would give the soufflé added richness, but you can certainly leave them out to make a virtually fat-free dessert. (A "normal" soufflé could contain 4 to 5 egg yolks.) The same is true for the chocolate, which makes a nice surprise to bite into. For heightened drama, I've included instructions for flambéing the soufflé, but you could omit this step, in which case you'd need only 3 tablespoons Grand Marnier. Be very careful when you flambé. Keep your face away from the pan and take care not to spill any of the flaming liquid on the tablecloth, the napkins, or your clothes.

Spray oil
½ cup sugar, plus 2 to 3 tablespoons
   for the ramekins
2 tablespoons cornstarch
2 teaspoons grated orange zest
1 cup skim milk
1 to 2 egg yolks (optional)
1 tablespoon orange marmalade

6½ tablespoons Grand Marnier
   (or other orange liqueur)
5 egg whites
½ teaspoon cream of tartar
1 to 2 ounces semisweet or bittersweet
   chocolate, cut into ¼-inch chunks
   (optional)

1. Lightly spray the insides (bottoms and sides) of eight 3-inch ramekins with spray oil. (Be sure to spray the inside rim.) Sprinkle the insides with sugar, rotating the ramekins to coat the bottom and sides with sugar. (Pour the sugar from one ramekin to another.) Preheat the oven to 400° F.

2. Combine 5 tablespoons of the sugar, 1 tablespoon of the cornstarch, and the orange zest in a small, heavy saucepan and whisk to mix. Gradually whisk in the milk in a thin stream. When all the ingredients are dissolved, place the pan over high heat and bring to a boil, whisking steadily: the mixture will thicken. Simmer for 2 minutes, whisking well.

3. Remove the pan from the heat and whisk in the egg yolk (if using) and the orange marmalade. Combine 2 tablespoons of the Grand

Marnier and the remaining 1 tablespoon corn-starch in a small bowl and mix to a smooth paste. Return the pan to the heat and bring the milk mixture just to a boil. Whisk in the Grand Marnier–cornstarch mixture and boil until thick. Remove the pan from the heat.

4. Beat the egg whites in a clean bowl at low speed for 1 minute. Add the cream of tartar. Gradually increase the speed to medium, then to medium-high, and beat the whites to soft peaks. Increase the speed to high, add the remaining 3 tablespoons sugar in a thin stream, and beat the whites until firm and glossy but not dry. Whisk ¼ of the whites into the hot Grand Marnier mixture. Fold this mixture into the remaining whites with a rubber spatula, working as gently as possible. (You don't want to deflate the whites.)

5. Spoon the soufflé mixture into the ramekins to fill halfway. Add the chocolate chunks and sprinkle in 1½ tablespoons of the Grand Marnier. Add the remaining soufflé mixture and smooth the tops with a wet spatula.

6. Bake the soufflés until puffed and nicely browned on the top and cooked in the center, 10 to 15 minutes. (To test for doneness, give one of the ramekins a gentle poke. The soufflé should wobble just a little.) Meanwhile, warm the remaining 3 tablespoons Grand Marnier in a small saucepan, but do not let boil. Serve the soufflé immediately. Touch a lighted match to the warm Grand Marnier and pour the flaming liquid on top. *Serves 8*

170 CALORIES PER SERVING; 4 G PROTEIN; 0 G FAT; 0 G SATURATED FAT; 32 G CARBOHYDRATE; 87 MG SODIUM; 0 MG CHOLESTEROL

FRUIT DESSERTS

DUET OF POACHED PEARS

There are two options for poaching liquid in this easy but elegant poached-pear recipe: a more traditional red-wine-and-port mixture, which will produce lovely rose-colored pears, and a lemon-and-Earl-Grey-tea-based mixture, which produces golden pears. Make one or the other, or some of both. As for the pears, I prefer Anjou or Comice, and they should be ripe but still firm. For heightened drama, you could serve the pears in Filo Nests (see page 33).

4 large pears
½ lemon

FOR ROSE-COLORED PEARS:
1 cup dry red wine
1 cup port
½ cup sugar
1 cinnamon stick
2 whole cloves
2 strips lemon zest
1½ teaspoons cornstarch
1 tablespoon water

FOR GOLDEN PEARS:
2 cups water
1 cup sugar
½ cup fresh lemon juice
2 tea bags Earl Grey tea
    (1½ tablespoons loose tea)
2-inch piece vanilla bean, split
1½ teaspoons cornstarch
1 tablespoon water

FOR THE GARNISH (OPTIONAL):
Fresh mint sprigs

1. Peel the pears, leaving the stems intact. Rub the peeled pears with the lemon to prevent them from discoloring and set aside.

2. To make rose-colored pears, put the wine, port, sugar, cinnamon stick, cloves, and zest in a narrow, deep nonreactive saucepan and bring to

Duet of Poached Pears in Filo Nests

a boil. Add the pears, reduce the heat, and gently simmer until tender, 10 to 15 minutes, turning with a slotted spoon to ensure even cooking. (To test for doneness, insert a metal skewer through the bottom of the pear to the center; it should pierce the pear easily.) Transfer the pears to a plate to cool, standing them upright. Continue simmering the poaching liquid until reduced to 1 cup. Dissolve the cornstarch in the water and stir it into the simmering liq-uid: it will thicken. Strain and let cool.

3. To make golden pears, follow the instructions for rose-colored pears, using the water, sugar, and lemon juice for the liquid and the tea bags and vanilla bean for the seasonings.

4. Arrange the poached pears on individual plates or a large platter. (If you are using Filo Nests, place one pear in each nest.) Spoon the sauce on top and garnish each pear with a sprig of mint, if desired.   *Makes 4 servings*

465 CALORIES PER SERVING; 1 G PROTEIN; 0.8 G FAT; 0 G SATURATED FAT; 110 G CARBOHYDRATE; 22 MG SODIUM; 0 MG CHOLESTEROL

MAPLE-AND-CRANBERRY-STUFFED BAKED APPLES WITH CIDER SAUCE

Baked apples are a classic New England dessert. My low-fat version uses apple butter and maple syrup to provide
the moistness traditionally supplied by butter. The acidity of the dried cranberries helps balance the sweetness.
Dried cranberries and maple sugar are available at gourmet shops and natural foods stores.
For a festive holiday dinner, serve the apples flambéed (see Note).

3 cups fresh apple cider
½ cup dried cranberries or raisins
8 large, firm, tart apples
6 gingersnap cookies or graham crackers,
    crumbed (about ¼ cup)
¼ cup packed maple sugar or light-brown
    sugar, or to taste

½ teaspoon ground cinnamon
3 tablespoons apple butter
1 teaspoon grated lemon zest
3 tablespoons maple syrup
2 teaspoons cornstarch
1 tablespoon dark rum

1. Warm the cider in a medium saucepan. Remove the pan from the heat and add the dried cranberries. Let sit 20 minutes.

2. Meanwhile, core the apples using an apple corer or melon baller, being careful not to cut all the way through the bottom: the idea is to create a cavity for the filling. Preheat the oven to 350° F.

3. Transfer the cranberries with a slotted spoon to a small mixing bowl, reserving the cider. Add the cookie crumbs, maple sugar, cinnamon, apple butter, and zest and stir to combine. Gently stuff this mixture into the apples, mounding it on top.

4. Using a skewer, make a dozen or so holes in the top of each apple and its mound of filling. Drizzle each apple with a little maple syrup. Place the apples in a baking dish and pour the reserved cider around them. Bake until the sides of the apples are soft, 40 to 60 minutes. If the filling starts to brown too much, cover the apples with foil.

5. Transfer the apples to shallow bowls. Strain the pan juices into a small saucepan and boil until reduced to 2 cups. Dissolve the cornstarch in the rum and whisk it into the pan juices. Bring to a boil: the sauce will thicken slightly. Pour the sauce over or around the apples and serve at once.

Note: To flambé the apples, heat 3 to 4 tablespoons rum in a small saucepan set over medium heat until warm to the touch (do not allow to boil). Touch a lighted match to the surface of the rum and pour the flaming liquid over the apples. Be very careful when you flambé. Keep your face away from the pan and take care not to spill any of the flaming liquid on the tablecloth, the napkins, or your clothes.

Makes 8 servings

210 CALORIES PER SERVING; 1 G PROTEIN; 1.8 G FAT; 0.1 G SATURATED FAT; 52 G CARBOHYDRATE; 21 MG SODIUM; 0 MG CHOLESTEROL

FRUIT SALSA

This fruit salsa makes a colorful accompaniment to cakes and pastries, not to mention a refreshing and healthy dessert in itself. Think of it as a turbo-charged fruit salad. Feel free to vary the fruits. Dried-Cherry Biscotti (see page 69) or Tortilla Crisps (see page 72) would make an excellent accompaniment.

1 cup diced fresh pineapple
(cut into ½-inch dice)
1 cup diced strawberries
(cut into ½-inch dice)
1 cup diced mango (cut into ½-inch dice)
(see Note)

2 tablespoons minced candied ginger or
2 teaspoons fresh
2 tablespoons fresh lime juice, or to taste
2 tablespoons packed light-brown sugar,
or to taste
½ cup slivered fresh mint leaves

Combine all the ingredients in a nonreactive mixing bowl and gently toss to mix. Correct the seasoning with lime juice or sugar as needed. The ingredients can be prepared ahead of time, but do not combine them more than 10 minutes before serving.

Note: To dice a mango, first peel it with a paring knife and cut the flesh off the seed. For a complete discussion of working with mangoes, see Note, page 52.   *Makes 4 to 6 servings*

85 CALORIES PER SERVING; 1 G PROTEIN; 0.5 G FAT; 0 G SATURATED FAT; 22 G CARBOHYDRATE; 4 MG SODIUM; 0 MG CHOLESTEROL

MANGO SOUP

The mango has been called the peach of the tropics. A ripe, juicy mango makes for one of the most luxurious eating experiences I know of. (Here in Florida, we like to say that the proper way to eat a mango is naked and in the bathtub!) This refreshing dessert soup makes a considerably more refined presentation, and it's a great way to use up stringy or fibrous mangoes.

3 cups diced ripe mango (2 to 3 mangoes)
⅓ cup confectioners' sugar, or to taste
2 tablespoons fresh lime juice, or to taste
1 cup fresh orange juice, plus more as needed
1 cup diced papaya (or more mango)
    (cut into ½-inch dice)

1 cup diced fresh pineapple
    (cut into ½-inch dice)
1 cup diced banana (cut into ½-inch dice)
3 tablespoons unsweetened shredded coconut,
    toasted (see Note, page 64)
3 tablespoons slivered fresh mint leaves

1. Purée the mango, sugar, and lime juice in a food processor. Add enough orange juice to obtain a pourable sauce. Correct the flavoring with sugar or lime juice. Force the sauce through a strainer into a large nonreactive mixing bowl, pressing with the back of a wooden spoon to extract the juice from the pulp. Discard the pulp.

2. Stir the diced papaya, pineapple, and banana into the mango sauce and carefully ladle the mixture into six large brandy snifters. Sprinkle the top with coconut and place a tuft of slivered fresh mint in the center. Serve with long-handled spoons.

Note: The best way to tell if a mango is ripe is by touch and smell: it should be squeezably soft and very fragrant. Some varieties remain green even when ripe. Let unripe mangoes ripen at room temperature. To dice a mango, first peel it with a paring knife and cut the flesh off the seed. To make peach soup, use 3 cups peeled and diced ripe peaches (2 to 3 peaches) instead of the mangoes.   *Serves 6*

162 CALORIES PER SERVING; 1.5 G PROTEIN; 3 G FAT; 0.1 G SATURATED FAT; 35 G CARBOHYDRATE; 17 MG SODIUM; 0 MG CHOLESTEROL

PEACH CRUMBLE

Is there anything more lasciviously luscious than a ripe peach at the height of the season?
But the following recipe could be used for making a crumble out of almost any fruit.

4 to 6 ripe peaches (enough to make
   6 cups fruit cut into ½-inch dice)
3 tablespoons pearl tapioca
¼ cup granulated sugar, or to taste
¼ cup light-brown sugar, packed
1 teaspoon cinnamon
Spray oil

FOR THE CRUMBLE TOPPING:
½ cup quick-cooking rolled oats
½ cup flour
½ cup packed light-brown sugar
1 to 2 tablespoons butter, melted
1 to 2 tablespoons canola oil
1 tablespoon peach schnapps or brandy

1. Preheat the oven to 400° F. Pit and dice the peaches. Toss the peaches with the tapioca, sugars, and cinnamon in a mixing bowl. If the mixture is too tart, add more sugar to taste. Spoon the peach mixture into a 6 × 10-inch gratin or baking dish that has been sprayed with spray oil.

2. Make the topping: Combine the oats, flour, brown sugar, butter, oil, and schnapps in the mixing bowl. Crumble the mixture with your fingers. Sprinkle it on top of the peaches.

3. Bake the crumble until the crust is brown and crisp and the peach mixture is thick and bubbly, 30 to 40 minutes. Spoon the crumble into shallow bowls for serving. (I like to serve hot crumble à la mode with frozen yogurt.)

Note: To pit a peach for dicing, make a cut around the circumference of the fruit to the pit. Twist the halves in opposite directions. This works best with freestone peaches; clingstones will have to be whittled off the pit.

Serves 6

356 CALORIES PER SERVING; 4 G PROTEIN; 5 G FAT; 1.5 G SATURATED FAT; 77 G CARBOHYDRATE; 29 MG SODIUM; 5 MG CHOLESTEROL

PUDDINGS, PARFAITS, AND FLANS

LEMON-YOGURT PARFAITS

The only difficult thing about making these stunning lemon parfaits is remembering to put the yogurt in the refrigerator to drain the night before. To make orange parfaits, substitute the Orange Curd in Note, page 56, for the Lemon Curd.

32 ounces plain nonfat yogurt
⅓ cup sugar, or to taste
1½ teaspoons grated lemon zest
1½ teaspoons vanilla extract
Lemon Curd (recipe follows)

FOR THE GARNISH (OPTIONAL):
Candied violets
Fresh mint sprigs

1. Using a yogurt strainer or a sieve lined with several layers of cheesecloth or paper towels and placed over a bowl, drain the yogurt in the refrigerator overnight.

2. Put the drained yogurt in a nonreactive bowl and whisk in the sugar, zest, and vanilla. Taste for sweetness, adding more sugar as desired. Bring to room temperature, then chill in the refrigerator.

3. Spoon the sweetened yogurt and the Lemon Curd into parfait glasses, alternating layers and smoothing each layer with the back of a spoon. The parfaits can be prepared up to 24 hours ahead. Just before serving, garnish with a candied violet and a mint sprig, if desired. *Makes 3 cups, which will serve 4*

355 CALORIES PER SERVING; 8 G PROTEIN; 2 G FAT; 0.5 G SATURATED FAT; 82 G CARBOHYDRATE; 104 MG SODIUM; 55 MG CHOLESTEROL

Lemon-Yogurt Parfaits

LEMON CURD

Remember lemon curd, that rich, tangy filling so laden with butter and egg yolk it could almost cause cardiac arrest? Here's a tangy version that contains only 1 egg (or 2, if you feel like splurging). It's so flavorful, you won't miss the fat.

1 cup sugar
1½ tablespoons cornstarch
1 or 2 eggs

1 cup fresh lemon juice (5 to 6 lemons)
4 teaspoons grated lemon zest

1. Put ½ cup of the sugar and the cornstarch in a nonreactive mixing bowl and whisk to combine. Whisk in the egg.

2. Put the lemon juice, the zest, and the remaining ½ cup sugar in a medium heavy nonreactive saucepan and bring to a boil. Whisk this in a thin stream into the egg mixture. Return the mixture to the saucepan and bring to a boil, whisking steadily. Reduce the heat and simmer 1 minute, or until thickened.

3. Transfer the Lemon Curd to a bowl and cover with plastic wrap, pressing it against the surface of the curd to prevent a skin from forming. Make a slit in the plastic wrap to allow the steam to escape. Let cool to room temperature, then refrigerate.

Note: To make Orange Curd, substitute ¾ cup fresh orange juice and ¼ cup fresh lime juice for the lemon juice, and 1 teaspoon grated orange zest for the lemon zest. Reduce the sugar to ½ cup and add it all in step 1.

Makes 1 cup, which will serve 4

227 CALORIES PER SERVING; 2 G PROTEIN; 1 G FAT; 0.4 G SATURATED FAT; 56 G CARBOHYDRATE; 17 MG SODIUM; 53 MG CHOLESTEROL

Dr. Spock's Apple Raspberry Pudding

Dr. Benjamin Spock is probably the world's most famous pediatrician. I met him at the restaurant Mark's in the Grove in Miami, where his wife, Mary, commandeered a corner of the kitchen to cook for her then ninety-two-year-old husband. The doctor credits his longevity, at least in part, to a strict macrobiotic diet that Mary cooks for him daily, even when they are on the road. This pudding is one of his favorite desserts. I've made a few embellishments to the recipe, including the use of apple cider instead of spring water.

2 cups fresh apple cider
1 cinnamon stick
½ teaspoon grated lemon zest
2 tablespoons agar-agar flakes (see Note)

1 Granny Smith apple, cored, quartered, and
 thinly sliced
1 to 2 tablespoons rice syrup (see Note)
1 cup fresh raspberries

1. Put the cider, cinnamon stick, zest, agar-agar, apple, and rice syrup in a medium heavy saucepan and bring to a boil. Reduce the heat and simmer until the agar-agar is dissolved, about 2 minutes. Off the heat, stir in the raspberries.

2. Remove and discard the cinnamon stick. Let the mixture cool slightly, then ladle it into wineglasses or glass custard cups. Refrigerate until set, about 2 hours, stirring once or twice to distribute the fruit throughout the pudding.

Note: This recipe is amazingly quick and easy to make, but it requires one or two special ingredients. Agar-agar is a seaweed-based gelling agent available at natural foods stores and Japanese markets. (Gelatin, which is made from animal bones, is not vegetarian.) Rice syrup is a natural sweetener; look for it at natural foods stores. The pudding may well be sweet enough for you without it or you can substitute honey as a sweetener. *Serves 4*

119 CALORIES PER SERVING; 1 G PROTEIN; 0.5 G FAT; 0 G SATURATED FAT; 32 G CARBOHYDRATE; 11 MG SODIUM; 0 MG CHOLESTEROL

CARIBBEAN PUMPKIN FLANS

Here's a Caribbean twist on that North American favorite, pumpkin pie. The traditional flan would be made with calabaza, a firm-fleshed Caribbean pumpkinlike squash (available at Hispanic and Caribbean markets and a growing number of supermarkets), but you could certainly use North American pumpkin or butternut or other squash. Vanilla, lemon zest, and caramel give this flan a flavor very different from that of traditional American pumpkin pie filling, but I think you'll see why it's enjoyed from one end of the Caribbean to the other. I like to make glasslike caramel shards to decorate the puddings.

FOR THE CARAMEL:
1½ cups sugar
Spray oil

FOR THE FILLING:
1 pound fresh pumpkin or other squash,
   peeled and cut into 1-inch cubes, or 1 cup
   canned pumpkin purée
1 cup evaporated skim milk

1 cup sweetened condensed skim milk
2 large eggs plus 4 large egg whites,
   or ⅔ cup egg substitute
1 teaspoon grated lemon zest
½ teaspoon ground cinnamon
Pinch salt (optional)
1 tablespoon dark rum
1 teaspoon vanilla extract

1. Put the sugar in a wide, shallow saucepan set over medium heat and cook until the sugar melts and turns dark brown. Pour 2 tablespoons of the caramel into each of 6 ramekins or custard cups, rotating the dish to coat the bottom and sides, and set aside to cool. (Take care to avoid being burned when handling the hot caramel.) Spray a baking sheet (preferably nonstick) with spray oil and pour on the remaining caramel, tilting the pan to create a broad puddle. Set aside to cool.

2. Preheat the oven to 350° F. and bring a kettle of water to a boil. If you are using canned pumpkin purée, proceed to step 3. If you are using fresh pumpkin, put the pieces in a saucepan set over medium heat and add water barely to cover. Simmer until very tender, 5 to 8 minutes. Drain the pumpkin well, then purée in a food processor or by pressing it through a strainer with a spatula. You should have about 1 cup.

3. Put the purée in a large mixing bowl. Whisk in the evaporated milk, condensed milk,

eggs, zest, cinnamon, salt, rum, and vanilla. Ladle this mixture into the caramel-lined ramekins.

4. Place the ramekins in a roasting pan, put the pan in the oven, and add boiling water to ½ inch. Bake until the flans are set, 20 to 30 minutes. To test for doneness, gently poke one of the ramekins. When the mixture no longer jiggles, it is done. Transfer the ramekins to a wire rack to cool to room temperature, then refrigerate until cold.

5. Place a shallow bowl or dessert plate over each ramekin and invert: the flan should slide right out. If it sticks, run the tip of a paring knife around the inside of each ramekin. Scrape off any remaining caramel and spoon it over and around the flan. Pry the caramel off the baking sheet and break it into 6 long, thin shards. Stand 1 shard in each flan and serve at once.

Makes 6 servings

421 CALORIES PER SERVING; 12 G PROTEIN; 2 G FAT; 0.7 G SATURATED FAT; 89 G CARBOHYDRATE; 162 MG SODIUM; 78 MG CHOLESTEROL

FROZEN DESSERTS

BAKED HAWAII

Here's my low-fat version of a dessert that was popular at hotel restaurants when I was a kid—baked Alaska. And what an extraordinary dessert it seemed at the time! Festooned with rococo swirls of meringue and served flambéed, it combined the best of both hot and cold desserts. My heart-healthy remake uses frozen yogurt instead of ice cream and fresh fruit instead of spongecake, but it sure doesn't lack for drama. Use your favorite flavor of frozen yogurt—I like cherry.

1 ripe pineapple with leaves attached
1 pint nonfat frozen yogurt or sorbet,
  softened
5 tablespoons rum or coconut rum (see Note)

FOR THE MERINGUE:
4 large egg whites, at room temperature
½ teaspoon cream of tartar
¾ cup sugar
3 tablespoons water
1 teaspoon vanilla extract

1. Using a large sharp knife, cut the pineapple in half lengthwise, starting at the end opposite the leaves and cutting through the leaves as well. Cut the core out of each pineapple half and discard. Remove the flesh with a grapefruit knife, being careful not to pierce the shell.

2. Cut the pineapple flesh into large dice. Put it in a nonreactive mixing bowl and stir in the frozen yogurt and 2 tablespoons of the rum.

Pack this mixture back into the pineapple shells and place them in the freezer.

3. Prepare the meringue: Put the egg whites in an electric mixer and start beating at low speed. Add the cream of tartar. Gradually increase the speed to medium and continue beating while you prepare the sugar syrup.

4. Place ½ cup of the sugar and the water in a small heavy saucepan with a lid. Cover and

Baked Hawaii

bring to a boil. Uncover and cook to the soft-ball stage.

5. Increase the mixer speed to high and beat the egg whites to soft peaks. Add the remaining ¼ cup sugar and beat until the whites are glossy and firm but not dry. This will take about 8 minutes in all. With the mixer running, pour the hot sugar syrup and vanilla into the egg whites and continue beating until completely cool.

6. Preheat the oven to 450° F. Transfer the meringue to a pastry bag fitted with a large star tip. Pipe decorative swirls of meringue over the top of the pineapple halves to completely en-case the frozen yogurt.

7. Place the pineapple halves on a baking sheet in the oven and bake until the meringue is nicely browned, 3 to 5 minutes. Transfer to a platter and serve at once. To flambé the Baked Hawaii, heat the remaining 3 tablespoons rum in a small saucepan set over medium heat until warm to the touch (do not allow to boil). Touch a lighted match to the surface of the rum and pour the flaming liquid over the pineapple halves. Be very careful when you flambé. Keep your face away from the pan and take care not to spill any of the flaming liquid on the table-cloth, the napkins, or your clothes.

Note: Coconut rum is actually a coconut-flavored rum and is available at most liquor stores. One popular brand is Malibu.

Makes 8 servings

169 CALORIES PER SERVING; 3 G PROTEIN; 0.3 G FAT; 0 G SATURATED FAT; 37 G CARBOHYDRATE; 80 MG SODIUM; 0 MG CHOLESTEROL

BALINESE BANANA SPLIT

This dish is inspired by a dessert I tasted in Bali called kolek pisang—*bananas in coconut-milk caramel. I've dramatically reduced the fat by using light coconut milk and skim milk instead of the full-fat coconut milk used in Bali. The cinnamon stick and lemongrass aren't strictly traditional, either, but they add a great flavor. I like to make this recipe with finger bananas or apple bananas (available at ethnic markets and some supermarkets), but regular bananas will work, too.*

½ cup packed dark-brown sugar
½ cup light coconut milk (see Note)
1 cup skim milk
1 cinnamon stick
1 stalk lemongrass, trimmed (see Note),
   or 2 strips lemon zest
12 finger bananas, 4 apple bananas, or 2
   regular bananas

2 teaspoons cornstarch
1 tablespoon water
1 pint vanilla nonfat frozen yogurt
2 tablespoons unsweetened shredded coconut,
   toasted (see Note)

1. Put the sugar in a large heavy saucepan (preferably nonstick) set over medium heat and, stirring with a wooden spoon, cook until it begins to smoke and turn dark brown. Remove the pan from the heat and add the coconut milk (be careful, as it may spatter). Return the pan to the heat and bring to a boil, stirring to dissolve the sugar. Stir in the skim milk and add the cinnamon stick and lemongrass. Reduce the heat and simmer, stirring from time to time to prevent scorching, until the mixture is richly flavored and you can taste the cinnamon and lemongrass, about 10 minutes.

2. Peel the bananas. If you are using apple bananas, cut them in half on the diagonal. If you are using regular bananas, cut them in thirds or quarters on the diagonal. Keep finger bananas whole. Add the bananas to the milk mixture and simmer until tender, 2 to 3 minutes. Mix the cornstarch with the water and add it to the saucepan. Simmer 1 minute: the sauce will thicken.

3. Divide the frozen yogurt among 4 bowls. Arrange the bananas on top and spoon the sauce around them. Sprinkle the banana splits with the shredded coconut and serve at once.

Note: To toast coconut, spread it on a piece of foil on a baking sheet and bake in a 350° F. oven 3 to 5 minutes, or until golden brown. Light coconut milk is a reduced-fat coconut milk available canned at gourmet shops. One good brand is A Taste of Thai. To trim lemongrass, cut off the dark-green leaves (about the top two-thirds). Strip off the outside layer of leaves.

Makes 4 servings

357 CALORIES PER SERVING; 7 G PROTEIN; 5 G FAT; 1.3 G SATURATED FAT; 71 G CARBOHYDRATE; 136 MG SODIUM; 1 MG CHOLESTEROL

CHOCOLATE SORBET

This rich, fudgy chocolate sorbet is the next best thing to chocolate ice cream. Think of it as a low-fat Carvel.

1¼ cups sugar
½ cup unsweetened Dutch-processed cocoa
   powder

2 cups water
2-inch piece vanilla bean, split
1 ounce unsweetened chocolate, chopped

1. Sift the sugar and cocoa into a large heavy saucepan. Gradually whisk in the water and add the vanilla bean. Bring the mixture to a rolling boil. Add the chocolate and whisk until melted. Let cool to room temperature, then refrigerate until cold.

2. Freeze the mixture in an ice-cream machine, following the manufacturer's instructions. Serve the sorbet in wineglasses or martini glasses.

Makes 3 cups, which will serve 4 to 6

285 CALORIES PER SERVING; 3 G PROTEIN; 5 G FAT; 1.7 G SATURATED FAT; 69 G CARBOHYDRATE; 11 MG SODIUM; 0 MG CHOLESTEROL

MANGO GELATO

*Milan meets Miami in this refreshing iced dessert. If you're a newcomer to the world of mangoes,
you may wish to read the note on page 52.*

3 cups diced ripe mango (2 to 3 mangoes)
1½ cups water
¾ cup sugar, or to taste

1 tablespoon minced candied ginger
2 tablespoons fresh lime juice, or to taste
Fresh mint sprigs, for garnish

1. Purée the mango in a food processor and force it through a strainer, pressing with the back of a wooden spoon. You should have about 2 cups of purée.

2. Put the water and sugar in a medium heavy saucepan and bring to a rolling boil. When the sugar is completely dissolved, remove the pan from the heat and let the syrup cool to room temperature.

3. Stir in the mango purée, ginger, and lime juice. Taste the mixture and add more sugar or lime juice as necessary.

4. Freeze the mixture in an ice-cream machine, following the manufacturer's instructions. To serve, spoon the gelato into martini glasses and garnish with a sprig of mint.

Makes about 1 quart, which will serve 6 to 8

144 CALORIES PER SERVING; 0.4 G PROTEIN; 0.2 G FAT; 0 G SATURATED FAT; 38 G CARBOHYDRATE; 5 MG SODIUM; 0 MG CHOLESTEROL

BEAUJOLAIS GRANITA

Granitas are the world's simplest frozen dessert, consisting of frozen sweetened wine or fruit juice flaked into icy crystals with a fork. (Granita means "small seed" in Italian—a fitting description of the tiny bits of ice that make up this grainy sorbet.) Few experiences can match the sensation of these delicate crystals melting on the tongue. This is a great way to use up those bottles of Beaujolais Nouveau you never got around to drinking in November.

1 bottle Beaujolais or other light, fruity red wine
1½ cups cold water

3 tablespoons fresh lemon juice
¾ cup sugar, or to taste

1. Put the wine, water, lemon juice, and sugar in a nonreactive mixing bowl and whisk until the sugar is completely dissolved. Transfer the mixture to a metal bowl and place in the freezer. As the liquid freezes, scrape it two or three times with a fork to break it up.

2. To serve, scrape again and spoon the granita into glasses that have been chilled in the freezer. Serve immediately, as the granita melts quickly.

Makes about 1 quart, which will serve 6 to 8

181 CALORIES PER SERVING; 0.5 G PROTEIN; 0 G FAT; 0 G SATURATED FAT; 27 G CARBOHYDRATE; 82 MG SODIUM; 0 MG CHOLESTEROL

FINGER FARE

DRIED-CHERRY BISCOTTI

Biscotti—the crisp, double-baked Italian cookies—have taken America by storm. For an offbeat touch, I flavor them with dried cherries, which are available at gourmet shops and natural foods stores or by mail order from American Spoon Foods, (800) 222-5886. For a New England accent, you could substitute dried cranberries.

2 large eggs plus 2 whites
½ cup granulated sugar
½ cup packed light-brown sugar
3 tablespoons canola oil
1 tablespoon kirsch or 1 teaspoon almond
   extract
2 teaspoons vanilla extract
1 cup dried cherries
2 teaspoons grated lemon zest

2¾ cups unbleached all-purpose flour,
   or as needed
¼ cup cornmeal (or more flour)
¼ cup cornstarch
¼ teaspoon salt (optional)
1½ teaspoons baking powder
1 teaspoon ground cardamom or cinnamon
Spray oil

1. Preheat the oven to 350° F. Combine the eggs, egg whites, sugars, oil, kirsch, and vanilla in a mixing bowl and stir with a wooden spoon to mix. Stir in the dried cherries and lemon zest. Sift in the flour, cornmeal, cornstarch, salt, baking powder, and cardamom and stir or beat just

Dried-Cherry Biscotti
Jake's Break-and-Eat Cookies
Lemon Crisp Cookies
Aunt Linda's Cinnamon-Currant Mandelbrot

to mix. You should wind up with a soft, pliable dough. Add more flour if dough is too sticky to handle.

2. Lightly spray a large baking sheet (preferably nonstick) with spray oil. Transfer the dough to the prepared baking sheet and roll it into a log about 16 inches long. Gently pat into a rectangle 5 to 6 inches wide and ½ inch high, tapering at the edges. (You may need to wet your hands to prevent the dough from sticking to them.) Score the top of each rectangle with a knife, making shallow cuts on the diagonal every ½ inch.

3. Bake the biscotti for 25 minutes, or until the top is firm to the touch. Remove the pan from the oven and let cool for 3 minutes.

4. Using a serrated knife, cut the loaf into ½-inch slices, following the lines you scored on top. Place the slices, cut side down, on the baking sheet and bake for 10 minutes. Turn the biscotti and bake for 10 minutes more, or until crusty.

5. Transfer the biscotti to a wire rack to cool to room temperature. Store in an airtight container.   *Makes about 3 dozen biscotti*

92 CALORIES PER PIECE; 2 G PROTEIN; 1.6 G FAT; 0.2 G SATURATED FAT; 18 G CARBOHYDRATE; 20 MG SODIUM; 12 MG CHOLESTEROL

AUNT LINDA'S CINNAMON-CURRANT MANDELBROT

Mandelbrot (literally, "almond bread") could be described as Jewish biscotti. This one features a crumbly cinnamon-sugar filling and is just the thing for dipping in coffee. Readers of my other books will be familiar with the culinary prowess of my Grammie Ethel. This recipe was inspired by her daughter, my aunt Linda Millison, from Philadelphia.

1½ cups sugar
1 teaspoon ground cinnamon
2 large eggs plus 2 large egg whites
¼ cup canola oil
2 teaspoons vanilla extract

1 teaspoon almond extract
¾ cup currants or raisins
3½ cups flour
2 teaspoons baking powder
Spray oil

1. Preheat the oven to 350° F. Mix ½ cup of the sugar with the cinnamon in a small bowl and set aside. Put the remaining 1 cup sugar, the eggs, and the egg whites in an electric mixer and beat at medium speed until light and foamy, about 5 minutes. Beat in the oil, vanilla, and almond extract. Stir in the currants. Sift the flour and baking powder into the mixture and stir just to combine. You should wind up with a soft, pliable dough. Add more flour if dough is too sticky to handle.

2. Lightly spray a baking sheet (preferably nonstick) with spray oil. Cut the dough in half. Roll each half into a log 14 inches long and 2 inches wide, and place it on the prepared baking sheet. (You may need to wet your hands to prevent the dough from sticking to them.) Using the side of your hand, make a 1-inch depression in the top running the length of the log. Sprinkle half the cinnamon-sugar into each depression and pinch the depression closed. Pat each log into a loaf shape about 12 inches long, 4 inches wide, and ¾ inch high.

3. Bake until the mandelbrot is firm to the touch and an inserted cake tester comes out clean, about 40 minutes. Transfer the loaves to a cutting board. Using a serrated knife, cut them into ½-inch slices. Transfer the slices to a wire rack to cool. Store the mandelbrot in an airtight container.

Makes about 4 dozen cookies

93 CALORIES PER PIECE; 1.7 G PROTEIN; 1.8 G FAT; 0.2 G SATURATED FAT; 18 G CARBOHYDRATE; 21 MG SODIUM; 11 MG CHOLESTEROL

TORTILLA CRISPS

Buñuelos, fried dough sprinkled with cinnamon-sugar, are a popular Mexican dessert. Here's a low-fat version made with flour tortillas and baked instead of deep-fried. The recipe is almost embarrassingly simple, requiring just 4 ingredients and 5 minutes' preparation time, but it never fails to delight.

4 flour tortillas
1 tablespoon butter, melted, or canola oil

⅓ cup sugar
1 tablespoon ground cinnamon

1. Preheat the oven to 400° F. Lightly brush the top of each tortilla with butter. Mix the sugar with the cinnamon in a small bowl.

2. Sprinkle 1 tablespoon of the cinnamon-sugar mixture over each tortilla and spread it evenly with a spoon. Cut each tortilla into 8 wedges. Transfer the wedges to a baking sheet lined with foil. Bake until the tortillas are crisp and lightly browned, about 5 minutes. Transfer the tortilla crisps to a wire rack to cool.

Makes 32 crisps

9 CALORIES PER PIECE; 0 G PROTEIN; 0.3 G FAT; 0.2 G SATURATED FAT; 2 G CARBOHYDRATE; 5 MG SODIUM; 1 MG CHOLESTEROL

LEMON CRISP COOKIES

These delicate cookies are modeled on a French confection called palets des dames. *They use a thoroughly non-French ingredient, however, Wondra flour, a gravy thickener that contains barley malt. (Look for it in cardboard cylinders in the flour section of your supermarket.) The idea for these cookies came from the baking guru Alice Medrich, who uses a similar mixture to make a low-fat pie crust.*

1 large egg plus 2 large egg whites
½ cup sugar
2 teaspoons grated lemon zest
1 teaspoon vanilla extract
3 tablespoons canola oil

1 cup Wondra flour
½ teaspoon baking powder
About 36 currants or dried cranberries
Spray oil

1. Preheat the oven to 350° F. Beat the egg, egg whites, sugar, lemon zest, and vanilla in an electric mixer at high speed until light and fluffy, about 3 minutes. Add the oil and beat 30 seconds. Add the Wondra flour and baking powder and beat just to mix.

2. Line a baking sheet with baking parchment or lightly spray it with spray oil. Using a spoon or a piping bag fitted with a ½-inch round tip, drop 1-inch mounds of batter on the baking sheet, leaving 3 inches between them. Tap the pan on a work surface to flatten the batter. Place a currant in the center of each cookie. Bake until the cookies are firm, about 20 minutes. Reduce the heat to 300° F. and bake the cookies until golden brown and crisp, 10 to 15 minutes more.

3. Remove the pan from the oven and transfer the cookies to a wire rack to cool.

Makes 3 dozen cookies

39 CALORIES PER COOKIE; 0.8 G PROTEIN; 1.3 G FAT; 0.1 G SATURATED FAT; 6 G CARBOHYDRATE; 9 MG SODIUM; 6 MG CHOLESTEROL

JAKE'S BREAK-AND-EAT COOKIES

These crisp, freeform cookies are the invention of my stepson, Jake Klein, who developed them for a Hong Kong restaurant we consulted for, called Miami Spice. (Yes, the restaurant was inspired by my cookbook, Miami Spice.) Jake likes to roll the cookies out in odd, jagged forms. If you feel like a klutz with a rolling pin, this recipe is for you!

1½ cups all-purpose flour, plus ¼ cup for
   rolling the cookies
6 tablespoons sugar, plus ¼ cup for rolling
   the cookies

1 scant teaspoon ground cardamom
⅛ teaspoon ground cloves
½ cup plain or vanilla nonfat yogurt, or more
   as needed

1. Preheat the oven to 350° F. Combine the 1½ cups flour, the 6 tablespoons sugar, and the spices in a mixing bowl or electric mixer fitted with a paddle. Stir in enough yogurt to obtain a soft, moist, pliable but rollable dough.

2. Liberally sprinkle a work surface with flour and sugar. Pinch off 1-inch pieces of dough and roll them into flat, freeform cookies. The dough will be quite sticky. Sprinkle the tops of the cookies with more flour and sugar as you roll them out. Transfer the cookies to nonstick baking sheets and bake until golden brown, 5 to 10 minutes. Transfer the cookies to a wire rack to cool. They'll crisp on cooling.

Makes 18 to 20 4-inch cookies

70 CALORIES PER COOKIE; 1.5 G PROTEIN; 0.2 G FAT; 0 G SATURATED FAT; 16 G CARBOHYDRATE; 5 MG SODIUM; 0 MG CHOLESTEROL

INDEX